Please return/renew this item by the
last date shown to avoid a charge.
Books may also be renewed by phone
and Internet. May not be renewed if
required by another reader.

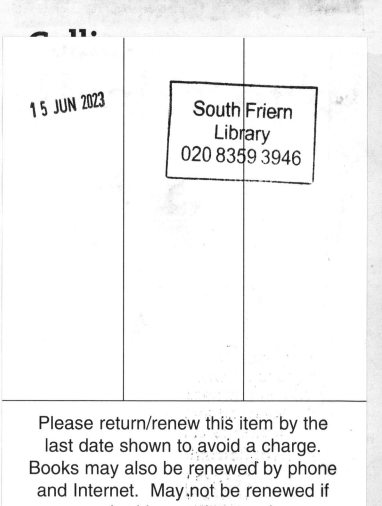

HarperCollins Publishers
Westerhill Road
Bishopbriggs
Glasgow
G64 2QT

First edition 2011

Reprint 10 9 8 7 6 5 4 3 2 1 0

© HarperCollins Publishers 2011

ISBN 978-0-00-736382-7

Collins ® is a registered trademark of
HarperCollins Publishers Limited

www.collinslanguage.com

A catalogue record for this book is
available from the British Library

Typeset by Davidson Publishing
Solutions, Glasgow

Printed in Great Britain by Clays Ltd,
St Ives plc

Editorial staff

American English consultant:
Orin Hargraves

Senior editors:
Penny Hands
Kate Woodford

Project management:
Lisa Sutherland

Contributors:
Sandra Anderson
Jennifer Baird
Katharine Coates

For the publisher:
Lucy Cooper
Kerry Ferguson
Elaine Higgleton

Computing support:
Thomas Callan

contents

contents

Collins Webster's Easy Learning English Verbs is designed for anyone who wants to improve their knowledge of English verbs and the way they work. Whether you are preparing for exams, need a quick look-up guide to English verbs, or you simply want to browse, *Collins Webster's Easy Learning English Verbs* offers you the information you require in a clear and accessible format.

A verb is a word that tells us about an action, an activity, a process, a state of being, or a state of mind. All grammatically complete sentences in English contain at least one verb. The form of a verb helps us to express some important ideas: the time the action is taking place, who carries it out, how likely it is that it will happen, how many people perform the action, and so on.

The first section of the book, called "What is a verb?", tells you more about tenses, the different grammatical forms of the verb, and how verbs work in a sentence.

The second section of the book contains dictionary entries of the most important types of verb. Most verbs in English are main verbs; these express actions and states. A special type of verb, called an auxiliary verb, is used in combination with a main verb to express ideas such as time, certainty, doubt, and completion. Some examples of auxiliary verbs are *be*, *do*, *have*, *can*, *could*, and *will*. Auxiliary verbs are explained in detail in the "key entries" in the dictionary section.

Phrasal verbs are also an important feature of English. English speakers use phrasal verbs in all contexts – not just in informal situations. The most common phrasal verbs are listed at the end of the entry for the verb they are related to. For example, the phrasal verbs *hang on* and *hang up* are listed under the entry for *hang*.

Some of the most useful English verbs are irregular. Irregular verbs are verbs that do not form the past simple tense and the past participle in the regular way. The most important irregular verbs are marked with a star in the dictionary section. There is also a list of the most common irregular verbs and their inflections on pages 246–247.

All explanations throughout the book are fully illustrated with examples of natural English taken from the Collins 4-billion-word corpus.

We hope you enjoy finding out more about this important area of the English language. For more information about Collins dictionaries, visit us at **www.collinslanguage.com**.

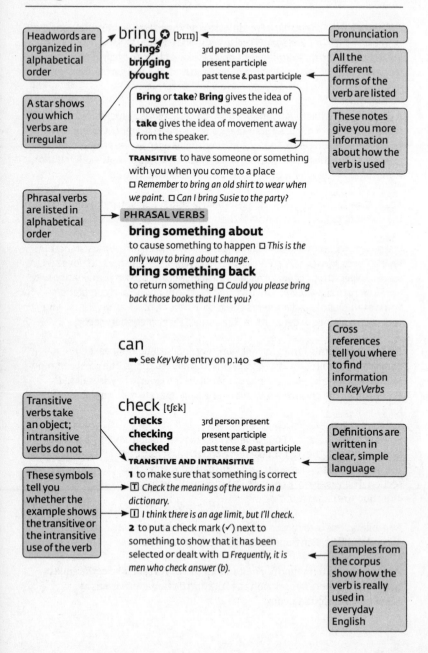

Headwords are organized in alphabetical order

A star shows you which verbs are irregular

Phrasal verbs are listed in alphabetical order

bring ✪ [brɪŋ]
brings   3rd person present
bringing   present participle
brought   past tense & past participle

Bring or **take**? **Bring** gives the idea of movement toward the speaker and **take** gives the idea of movement away from the speaker.

TRANSITIVE to have someone or something with you when you come to a place
□ *Remember to bring an old shirt to wear when we paint.* □ *Can I bring Susie to the party?*

PHRASAL VERBS

bring something about
to cause something to happen □ *This is the only way to bring about change.*

bring something back
to return something □ *Could you please bring back those books that I lent you?*

Pronunciation

All the different forms of the verb are listed

These notes give you more information about how the verb is used

can
➡ See *Key Verb* entry on p.140

Cross references tell you where to find information on *Key Verbs*

Transitive verbs take an object; intransitive verbs do not

These symbols tell you whether the example shows the transitive or the intransitive use of the verb

check [tʃɛk]
checks   3rd person present
checking   present participle
checked   past tense & past participle
TRANSITIVE AND INTRANSITIVE
1 to make sure that something is correct
Ⓣ *Check the meanings of the words in a dictionary.*
Ⓘ *I think there is an age limit, but I'll check.*
2 to put a check mark (✓) next to something to show that it has been selected or dealt with □ *Frequently, it is men who check answer (b).*

Definitions are written in clear, simple language

Examples from the corpus show how the verb is really used in everyday English

We have used the International Phonetic Alphabet (IPA) to show how the words are pronounced. The symbols used in the International Phonetic Alphabet are shown in the table below.

IPA symbols

Vowel sounds

ɑ	calm, drop, fall.
ɑː	draw, saw.
æ	act, mass, lap.
ai	drive, cry, lie.
aiər	fire, tire, buyer.
au	out, down, loud.
auər	flour, tower, sour.
e	met, lend, pen.
ei	say, main, weight.
eᵊr	fair, care, wear.
ɪ	fit, win, list.
i	feed, me, beat.
iᵊr	cheer, hear, clear.
ou	note, phone, coat.
ɔ	more, cord, sort.
ɔi	boy, coin, joint.
ʊ	could, stood, hood.
u	you, use, choose.
jʊᵊr	sure, pure, cure.
ʃɜr	turn, third, word.
ʌ	but, fund, must.
ə	(the weak vowel in) about, account, cancel.

Consonant sounds

b	bed
d	done
f	fit
g	good
h	hat
j	yellow
k	king
l	lip
m	mat
n	nine
p	pay
r	run
s	soon
t	talk
v	van
w	win
x	loch
z	zoo
ʃ	ship
ʒ	measure
ŋ	sing
ŋ	cheap
θ	thin
ð	then
ðʒ	joy

Notes

Primary and secondary stress are shown by marks above and below the line, in front of the stressed syllable. For example, in the word *abbreviation*, /əˌbriːviˈeɪʃən/, the second syllable has secondary stress and the fourth syllable has primary stress.

What is a verb?

What is a verb?

A **verb** tells us about an action, an activity, a process, a state of being, or a state of mind. Ordinary verbs are called **main verbs**.

> *This basket **holds** quite a lot.*
> *Helen **feels** much happier now.*
> *I **forgot** that it **was** your birthday.*
> *Paul **owned** several old motorbikes.*

A special group of verbs are called **auxiliary verbs**. They work together with main verbs.

> *I **am** thinking.*
> *She **has** seen the film already.*
> *I **can** help you.*
> *We **might** need to get help.*

Main verbs

These are the verbs that we use to indicate actions and states. Most of the verbs in English are main verbs. They are also called **lexical** verbs. Main verbs are divided or **classified** in several ways:

- according to whether they refer to **states**
  *I **can** really **taste** the herbs in this omelet.*
  *This scarf **belongs** to me.*
  *He **hates** losing.*
  *She always **liked** boats and sailing.*
  *I already **feel** that I **have known** you for ages.*

– or **actions**.

> Three boys **were kicking** a ball around in the field.
> We **were running** across the football field.
> For six hours, Stuart **drove** across open desert.

– into **regular** and **irregular** verbs according to the spelling of their forms.

> regular: talk, talks, talking, talked.
> irregular: swim, swims, swimming, swam, swum.
> irregular: go, goes, going, went, gone.

– according to whether or not they are followed by an object: that is, whether they are **transitive** or **intransitive**. See p. 6.

> I **can read**.
> We both **read** the same newspaper.
> **Don't tell** me.
> We both **ran** away.
> Sue **found** a bracelet.
> I **saw** my best friend on Friday.

Auxiliary verbs

These verbs are used in combination with main verbs in order to allow us to talk about different times or periods of time, different degrees of completion, and different amounts of certainty or doubt. There are several types of auxiliary verb. The **primary** auxiliaries help express time, and the **modal** auxiliaries help to express certainty and doubt. See pp. 16–23.

The verb phrase

Sentences consist of a number of parts, using different parts of speech. One of these is the **verb phrase**, which includes the main verb, and which may have auxiliary verbs with it. In a sentence, you usually put the verb phrase immediately after the subject. When a verb phrase consists of a single word it is called a **simple** verb. Many verb phrases in English are made by combining an auxiliary verb and a main verb. See also pp. 16–19.

> *The girls **had been swimming**.*
> *The new teacher **came** in.*
> *They **had finished**.*
> *She **uses** her skateboard quite a bit.*
> *Rajiv **was reading** a new novel.*
> *She **is riding** someone else's horse.*

Direct and indirect objects

The **object** of a verb (if there is one) normally comes after the verb phrase. Whether there is an object or not depends on the meaning of the verb. For example, if you want to talk about what someone is doing, you might say "*She is writing*" but if you want to talk about the point of the activity, you might say, "*She is writing a book*".

> *She was riding.*
> *She was riding **her horse**.*
> *Erica was writing.*
> *Erica was writing **a letter***.

An object that follows a verb like this is called the **direct object**.

> *Rory found **a pen***.
> *Our cat doesn't like **milk***.

Some verbs also have another sort of object, called an **indirect object**. An indirect object names the person for or to whom something is done. It is usually needed with verbs like *give, find,* and *owe*. For example, with *give,* we need to name both the thing that is given and the person it is given to.

> *Mike owes **Tom** **five dollars***.
> *Rob gave **me** **a box of chocolates***.
> *Susan bought **her rabbit** **some more food***.

Transitivity

Some verbs must always take a direct object, some never take a direct object; others sometimes take one and sometimes don't, depending on the meaning. When a verb has an object it is called a **transitive** verb. Transitive verbs are often connected with: physical objects (*build, catch, sell, wear*); senses (*feel, hear*); feelings (*enjoy, frighten, hate, surprise*); facts or ideas (*believe, forget, include*); or people (*blame, convince, persuade, please*).

> Rowan bought *a magazine*.
> I don't like *rap music*.

A verb that does not have an object is called an **intransitive** verb. These often refer to: existence (*appear, die, live*); the human body (*ache, blush, smile*); human noises (*cough, cry, snore, speak*); light, smell, or vibration (*glow, sparkle, throb*); or position or movement (*arrive, fall, go, run, stand, wait*).

> Lynn fainted.
> Patrick screamed.
> Soon, everyone was shouting.

Some verbs may be either **transitive** or **intransitive**.

> Ann was reading (a letter).
> Ravi was drawing (a picture).

When a verb has both an indirect and a direct object it is called a **ditransitive** verb.

> Amy owes **Mark ten dollars**.
> Stephen gave **me some flowers**.
> Katie bought **her hamster a new cage**.

- Some verbs must have an adverbial as well as a direct object for example, to specify a place.

> He placed **the package on the chair**.
> She put **the umbrella in a corner**.

Reflexive verbs

Transitive verbs are used with a reflexive pronoun to indicate that the object is the same as the subject.

> I hurt **myself**.

The **reflexive pronouns**:

person	singular	plural
1st	myself	ourselves
2nd	yourself	yourselves
3rd masculine	himself	themselves
3rd feminine	herself	themselves
3rd neuter	itself	themselves
general		oneself

Reflexive pronouns are used:

– when the speaker or writer is referring to an action that he or she has caused to happen and of which he or she is also the object.

> I cut **myself** with the carving knife.
> Sometimes I just don't like **myself** very much.

– when the direct object or prepositional object of a sentence has the same reference as the subject.

> John looked at **himself**.
> John taught **himself** to play the guitar.

The formal reflexive pronoun **oneself** can be used to refer to people in general. More informally, **yourself** is used in the same way.

> The first rule is not to take **oneself** too seriously. (formal)
> The first rule is not to take **yourself** too seriously. (informal/standard)

Oneself can also be used as a substitute for the 1st person singular. If it is used like this, the subject pronoun should be *one*. This is a formal use and is not common in everyday speech.

> *One asks **oneself** whether it is worth the bother.*
> *One owes it to **oneself** to do something worthwhile.*

Some verbs take a reflexive pronoun only in particular uses of the verb.

> *Jeremy introduced **himself**.* *The cat washed **itself**.*

You can leave out the reflexive pronoun if it is obvious that the subject was performing the action of the verb on him- or herself.

> *Jeremy **washed** and **dressed**, then went out.*

When a preposition is followed by a pronoun, the pronoun is normally in the object form.

> *They all looked at **him** in silence.*

If that pronoun refers to the subject of the main verb, however, it must be a reflexive pronoun.

> *She looked at **herself** in the mirror.*

- The reflexive can be used to make something you say stronger. To make a strong point, we sometimes use a normal subject or object pronoun and a reflexive pronoun as well.

> *He told me **himself** that he was leaving.* *I'll do it **myself**.*

- The reflexive can also be used with or without *by* meaning "alone" or "without help".

> *I think you should try and do it **yourself**.*
> *Did she do that all by **herself**?*

Reciprocal verbs

Some verbs are used for talking about actions that involve two people doing the same thing to each other. These verbs are sometimes called reciprocal verbs.

> We **met** in Delhi.
> They **hugged**.

The two people involved in the action are often mentioned as the plural subject of the verb, and the verb does not have an object. For example, *John and Mary argued* means that John argued with Mary and Mary argued with John.

> We **competed** furiously.
> Their children **are always fighting**.

When you want to show that both people are equally involved, you can use the pronouns *each other* or *one another* as the object of the verb. Verbs that are used for talking about actions in which there is physical contact between people are often used with *each other* or *one another*.

> We **embraced each other**.
> They **fought one another** desperately for it.
> They **touched one another**.

Some verbs do not take an object, so you use a preposition before *each other* or *one another*.

> They **parted from each other** after only two weeks.
> We **talk to one another** as often as possible.

With some verbs you have a choice of preposition before *each other* or *one another*. For example, you can *fight with* one another or *fight against* one another.

*Many countries are **competing with each other**.*
*Did you **compete against each other** in yesterday's race?*
*Stephen and I spent the evening **talking to one another***
about old times.
*They talked **with one another** for about ten minutes.*

With some verbs, you can only use *with* before *each other* or *one another*.
Note that most of these verbs are used for talking about people talking
or working together.

*We do **agree with each other** sometimes.*
*Have they **communicated with each other** since then?*
*The two trucks **collided with one another** on the freeway.*

Linking verbs

Some verbs are followed by a **complement** rather than an object. These verbs are called **linking verbs**:

> *appear   be   become   feel   get   go   grow   keep   look*
> *prove   remain   seem   smell   sound   stay   taste   turn*

The **subject complement** is a word or phrase that tells us more about the subject.

> Alan is *a nice person*.
> Ricardo is *a nurse*.
> Alison seems *very happy*.
> That's *it*!

The subject complement is linked to the subject by a verb, and the order is:

> **subject + verb + subject complement**

Subject complements can be noun phrases, pronouns, adjectives, or even prepositional phrases.

- Most adjectives can be used after a group of verbs that includes: *appear, be, become, look, seem, smell, taste*, etc. An adjective that is used in this position is called a **predicative** adjective and it is functioning as a **complement**.

  > The tickets seemed *expensive*, but the show was *excellent*.
  > These little cakes are *delicious*.

*Soon afterwards, Patrick became **ill***.
*Jackie appeared **friendly enough** when I first met her.*

Less frequently we find an **object complement**. The object complement tells us more about the direct object. It relates directly to the object and is placed after it. Verbs that can take an object complement with their direct object include *make*, *call*, and *appoint*. The word order is:

> **subject + verb + direct object + object complement**

*Peter's phone call made **Maureen** happy.*
*She called **me** a fool.*
*They appointed **him** Director.*

Irregular verbs

Irregular verbs are verbs that *do not* form the past simple tense and the past participle by adding **-ed** to the base form. For a list of irregular verbs and their inflections, see pp. 248–249.

The three main groups of irregular verbs

In Group A, the base form, the past simple and the past participle are the same:

1	the base form	***put***
2	the present simple	*puts*
3	the past simple	***put***
4	the present participle	*putting*
5	the past participle	***put***

A

bet	*cut*	*let*	*shed*	*spread*
burst	*hit*	*put*	*shut*	*thrust*
cast	*hurt*	*set*	*split*	*upset*

In Group B, the past simple and the past participle have the same form:

1	the base form	***buy***
2	the present simple	*buys*
3	the past simple	***bought***
4	the present participle	*buying*
5	the past participle	***bought***

B1

base form	past form	base form	past form
bend	bent	hang	hung
bind	bound	have	had
bleed	bled	hear	heard
bring	brought	keep	kept
build	built	kneel	knelt
buy	bought	lay	laid
catch	caught	make	made
find	found	say	said

Some of these verbs have alternative spellings for the past participle:

B2 The past form may be either *a* or *b*.

base form	past forms
burn	burnt, burned
dream	dreamt, dreamed
leap	leapt, leaped
learn	learnt, learned

In Group C, the base form, the past simple, and the past participle all have different forms:

1	the base form	**go**
2	the present simple	goes
3	the past simple	**went**
4	the present participle	going
5	the past participle	**gone**

C

base form	past forms	base form	past forms
arise	arose arisen	ring	rang rung
awake	awoke awoken	rise	rose risen
bear	bore borne	saw	sawed sawn
begin	began begun	see	saw seen
bite	bit bitten	shake	shook shaken
blow	blew blown	show	showed shown
break	broke broken	shrink	shrank shrunk
fly	flew flown	strive	strove striven
give	gave given	take	took taken
know	knew known	throw	threw thrown
ride	rode ridden	write	wrote written

Auxiliary verbs

An auxiliary verb is a verb that is used together with a main verb.

- **Be** and **have** are the **primary auxiliaries**.

- **Be** is used to make the present continuous and the past continuous.

    > I **am working**.
    > Rob **is using** the computer.
    > We **were** all **wondering** about that.
    > Kevin **was teaching** in Argentina in 1985.

    and also the passive.

    > These books **are sold** in supermarkets.
    > Martin **was arrested** and held overnight.

- **Have** is used to make the present perfect and the past perfect.

    > Stephen **has finished** fixing the car.
    > George and Alice **have seen** the show already.
    > Amanda **had** already **eaten** when we arrived.
    > They **had** not **expected** to see us there.

- **Do** is the **supporting auxiliary** (see pp. 158–163). It is used in forming negatives, questions, and emphatic statements. See pp. 87, 89–90, 102–105.

    > I **do** not **like** sausage at all.
    > **Do** you **like** shrimp?
    > You **do like** shrimp, don't you?

- **Will**, **may**, **might**, and the other verbs covered on pp. 20–23 are the **modal auxiliary verbs**, usually called simply **modal verbs** or **modals**. A modal verb allows us to talk about actions as possible, certain/uncertain, or necessary.

*Charlie **will go** home on Friday.*
*Charlie **may go** home on Friday.*
*Charlie **could go** home on Friday.*
*Charlie **must go** home on Friday.*

Auxiliaries can be combined together in a single verb phrase. For example, a verb phrase may consist of a **modal** + a form of *have* + a form of *be* + a form of a **main verb**.

> *I **could have been making** a bad mistake by trusting him.*
> *Sara **will have been living** in New Mexico for 2 years next month.*
> *You **must have been given** the wrong number.*

The auxiliary verb, or if there is more than one of them, the first auxiliary verb, has the following grammatical functions.

– It shows **tense**.
  *I **have** seen it.*
  *She **had** seen it.*
  *She **has** been thinking.*
  *She **had** been thinking.*

– It shows **number** and **person** agreement with the subject.
  ***She has** seen it.*
  ***They have** seen it.*
  ***I am** looking for it.*
  ***You are** looking for it.*

– It will take any **negative** immediately after it.
  *I **do not** want to do that.*
  *She **has never** been good at concentrating.*

– It can come before the subject to make a **question**.
  ***Do you** want to help us?*
  ***Have you** got a cell phone?*

Contracted forms

Auxiliaries are very often used in contracted forms, e.g., *I'm*, *I've*, *we'd*, *Sue's* (= *Sue has* or *Sue is*).

> **We're** back! (**We are** back!)
> **I've** found it. (**I have** found it.)
> **They'd** gone when I got there. (**They had** gone when I got there.)
> **Tom's** here. (**Tom is** here.)

The contracted negative form **auxiliary + n't** is common with all the auxiliaries except *am*, e.g., *hasn't*, *wouldn't*, *don't*.

> She **isn't** (is not) trying.
> We **don't** (do not) live here.
> He **hasn't** (has not) seen it.
> I **can't** (cannot) come.

In most modern dialects of English (including American and British), the contracted form of ***am not***, when it is part of a question, is ***aren't I***.

> **Aren't I** going to need some matches?
> I'm getting a ride with you, **aren't I**?

- Contracted forms are more informal than full forms. They are therefore more common in spoken English. Full forms are usually preferred in formal written English.

Auxiliaries are used in sentence tags. See pp. 98–101 for more about sentence tags.

> You had just bought that carpet when the kitchen flooded,
>   **hadn't you**?
> It's Katie's birthday on Saturday, **isn't it**?
> You are joking, **aren't you**?

Auxiliaries are also used to make a short addition to a statement, such as:

- a positive addition to a positive statement, with *so* or *too*.

  *I went to the park and Lucy **did too**.*
  *I loved the movie, and **so did** Fred.*

- a negative addition to a negative statement, with *neither* or *nor*.

  *My dad never eats mussels and **neither do** I.*
  *I don't want to speak to William now. – **Nor do** I.*
  *I can't understand it. – **Neither can** I.*

Auxiliaries can be used in positive sentences to show emphasis. When they show emphasis they are never contracted.

  *You **have** made a mess!*
  *That **was** a nice surprise!*
  *I **am** proud of Katie. She's so clever.*

In the present simple tense and the past simple tenses the appropriate form of ***do*** is used to show emphasis.

  *I **do like** Perry. – So do I.*
  *We **did have** a great time.*

> An auxiliary can be used on its own to give a short answer to a question. Whatever auxiliary is used in the question is used on its own in the answer. The main verb is not repeated. Short answers are very common in spoken English.
>
> ***Do** you like avocados? Yes, I **do**./No, I **don't**.*
> ***Have** you read anything by Michael Crichton?*
>   *Yes, I **have**./No, I **haven't**.*

Modal verbs

Modal verbs are a special kind of **auxiliary** verb.

> *Look, I **can** do it! – Oh yes! So you **can**.*
> ***Can** I use your phone? – Of course you **can**.*
> *Do you think she **will** come? – I'm sure she **will**.*
> *I **must** get our tickets today.*

Modal verbs are used when you need to add special elements of meaning to a main verb, e.g.;

– to express different degrees of doubt and possibility about the action of the main verb.

> *I **may** not **be able** to do it.*
> *I think that I **might have caught** your cold.*
> *I **could ask** for you, if you like.*
> *You **couldn't do** it, **could** you?*

– to express degrees of future possibility, for example, the definite future, **will**, the possible future, **may**, and the conditional future, **could**.

> *You **will be seeing** her on Friday at Jackie's house.*
> *I **may be** late coming home tomorrow evening.*
> *I **could bring** some more bread home with me tonight.*

– to request or give permission for an action to take place.

> ***May** I come in?*
> *You **can** borrow my car tonight if you like.*

– to make a prohibition, when used with a negative.

> *You **shouldn't** use this computer without permission.*
> *You **cannot** borrow my car tonight.*
> *He **must not** see this letter.*

- to speculate.

   *The weather's so bad the flight **could** be late.*
   *It **might** be all over by the time we get there.*
   *He **may** be very upset about all this.*

- to express obligation and duty.

   *I **must** hand in my essay today.*
   *Hector **ought to** tell the truth.*

- to refer to typical behavior.

   *She **can** be very kind on occasions like this.*

- to add politeness to a request which might otherwise sound rude.

   ***Would you** please close the door?*

Modals can all be used for future reference, especially when they are used with a time adverbial. See pp. 63–69.

   *You **will be seeing** her **on Friday** at Jackie's house.*
   *I **may be** late home **tomorrow evening**.*
   *I **could bring** some more bread home with me **tonight**.*

Some modals can be used for talking about an indefinite past time. They can refer to an action that was done frequently in the past when they are used with a time adverbial.

   *When I was little, I **would** ride my bike around and around the yard.*

Form

Unlike other verbs, modal verbs have only one form, the **base form**, and only one tense, the present simple.

   *You **will** be seeing her on Friday at Jackie's house.*
   *I **may** be late getting home tomorrow evening.*
   *I **might** go to visit Grandma on Saturday.*

They do not have a *to* infinitive. They have no **-s** inflection in the 3rd person singular.

> **He will** be seeing her on Friday.
> **She may** be late getting home.

- Since modal verbs do not have past tense forms, you have to use other verbs to provide some of the modal meanings in the past. For example, past necessity is expressed by *had to* instead of *must*. See also p. 184.

> I **must** visit Aunt May today.
> I **had to** visit Aunt May yesterday.

- The modals **shall** and **will** are usually contracted to **'ll** in spoken English. All the negative forms can be contracted to form a single word such as **can't**, **won't**, **wouldn't**. These contracted forms are common in both spoken and written English.

> I will/shall = **I'll**
> We will/shall = **we'll**
> You **mustn't** say things like that, Jane.
> John **can't** come to my party.

There are other contracted forms such as **he'll**, **we'll**, and **they'll**, which are common in spoken English but rare in written English.

- There are some verbs that act as modals sometimes and as full main verbs at other times. These are called **semi-modal verbs**. See also pp. 150–155.

> How **dare** he!
> He **dared** to ask me to do his laundry!
> She **needn't** come if that's how she feels.
> Monica **needs** a new raincoat.

Position

Modals come before any other auxiliary verb or main verb in the verb phrase.

- Modal verbs are followed by the **base form** of the verb if there is no other auxiliary verb.

  *Yes, you **can borrow** those earrings tonight.*
  *You **should try** that new restaurant in town.*
  *You **must come** over again some time.*

- If one of the auxiliary verbs ***have*** or ***be*** follows the modal verb, the main verb will take the appropriate present or past participle form.

  *I **may have upset** him.*
  *You **could have looked** for it yourself.*
  *Janice **might be coming** too.*
  *Sue **will have been worried** about her, I imagine.*

- In negative sentences, ***not*** or any other negative word comes immediately after the modal verb and in front of all the other verbs.

  *They **may not wait** for you if you're late.*
  *He **must never be** disturbed after 9 o'clock.*

- ***Can*** cannot be combined with the auxiliary form ***have***; use ***could*** instead. The negative form ***can't*** can be combined with ***have***.

  *They **can't have seen** him.*   **but not** ~~*They can have seen him*~~.
  *They **could have seen** him.*

Phrasal verbs

A **phrasal verb** is a type of verb that is created when a main verb is combined with either:

– an **adverb**,

> *take off*   *give in*
> *blow up*   *break out*

– a **preposition**,

> *look after* (someone)   *turn into* (something)

– or an **adverb** + **preposition**,

> *put up with* (something)   *get away with* (something)

Type A. Verb + adverb

Some Type A phrasal verbs have no object; they are **intransitive**. The sentence makes sense without any addition to the verb.

> *Mary **went away**.*
> *Herman **sat down**.*
> *The students **came back**.*

Others do require an object; these phrasal verbs are **transitive**.

> *We could **make out** a figure in the distance.*
> *He tried to **blow up** the aircraft.*
> *Could you **put** your clothes **away**, please?*

If the object is a **noun**, many Type A phrasal verbs will allow the adverb to come either:

– before the object,

> I **picked up** Jim *on my way home*.
> He **blew out the candle**.
> She **put away her things**.

– or after the object.

> I **picked** Jim **up** *on my way home*.
> He **blew the candle** *out*.
> She **put her things** *away*.

If the object is a **pronoun**, the pronoun must come before the adverb.

> I **picked** him **up**.
> He **blew** it **out**.
> She **put** them *away*.

Sometimes you can guess the meaning of these verbs from the meanings of their parts.

> to **sit down** = *sit + down*
> to **go away** = *go + away*

Sometimes you have to learn the new meanings, or use a dictionary.

> to **make up** *(an answer)* = *invent*
> to **turn down** *(an invitation)* = *decline*
> to **work out** *(a problem)* = *solve*
> to **put up** *(a visitor)* = *accommodate*

Type B. Verb + preposition

Type B phrasal verbs always have an object. This is because prepositions always have an object.

> He **asked for** the check.
> He **asked for** it.
> She **listened to** the doctor.
> She **listened to** her.
> They **referred to** our conversation.
> They **referred to** it.

Sometimes there are two objects – the object of the verb and the object of the preposition.

> He **asked** the waiter **for** the check.

Type C. Verb + adverb and preposition

Type C phrasal verbs are a combination of the two previous kinds of verb. All the parts of a Type C phrasal verb come before the object.

> We are **looking forward to** our vacation.
> We are **looking forward to** it.
> Don't **put up with** bad behavior.
> Don't **put up with** it.
> You must **look out for** the warning signs.
> You must **look out for** them.

• It is sometimes hard to tell adverbs and prepositions apart, because often the same word can be both a preposition and an adverb, depending on how it is used.

The following are examples of the three types of phrasal verb that are explained above.

Type A

Phrasal verbs made from a verb + an adverb may be intransitive (= they do not take an object) or transitive (= they take an object).

some phrasal verbs that do not take an object	some phrasal verbs that do take an object
to break down	to blow something up
to carry on	to break something off
to fall down	to bring a child up
to get around	to bring a subject up
to get up	to cheer somebody up
to give up	to clear something up
to go away	to close something down
to go off	to give something up
to go on	to leave something out
to grow up	to make something up
to hold on	to pick someone up

Type B

Phrasal verbs made from a verb + a preposition are all transitive.

to add to something	to hope for something
to agree with someone	to insist on something
to apply for a job	to laugh at something
to approve of something	to listen to something
to arrive at a place	to look for something
to ask for something	to look into something
to believe in something	to look over something
to belong to someone	to pay for something
to call on someone	to refer to something
to care for someone	to rely on someone
to come across something	to run into someone
to deal with something	to run over something

Some Type B verbs are doubly transitive, since both the verb and the preposition can have an object.

> to **ask** a grown-up **for** help
> to **check** your answers **with** the teacher
> to **pay** the cashier **for** your shopping items
> to **refer** a customer **to** the manager

Type C
Phrasal verbs with an adverb plus a preposition all take a prepositional object.

to be fed up with something	to keep away from something
to break in on someone	to lead up to something
to carry on with something	to look back on something
to catch up with something	to look forward to something
to check up on something	to look out for something
to come up with something	to look up to someone
to cut down on something	to make up for something
to do away with something	to put in for something
to face up to something	to run away with something
to fall back on something	to run out of something
to get on with something	to run up against something
to get out of something	to stand up for something
to go back on something	to walk out on someone
to go in for something	to watch out for something

Introduction to tense

We use verbs to talk about actions and states. Verb **tenses** allow us to indicate the time when the action or state takes place. All main verbs have two **simple** tenses, the **present simple** and the **past simple**.

present simple	past simple
I walk she sings they come you bring	I walked she sang they came you brought

In these tenses the verb is used on its own without any auxiliary verbs.

English verbs also have **present** and **continuous** forms. In these forms the main verb is accompanied by one or both of the auxiliary verbs **be** (see pp. 122–126) and **have** (see pp. 174–181). See pp. 39–69 for more on tense.

Aspect

There are two ways of expressing **aspect** in English – the **continuous** and the **perfect** forms.

- The term **aspect** is used to talk about continuing actions compared with completed actions or states. Simple tenses do not have aspect.

continuing actions	
I am walking she is singing they are coming you are bringing	I was walking she was singing they were coming you were bringing

> *completed actions*
>
> | | |
> |---|---|
> | *I have walked* | *I had walked* |
> | *she has sung* | *she had sung* |
> | *they have come* | *they had come* |
> | *you have brought* | *you had brought* |

We use these forms when we want to talk about:

– the continuous nature of an action (using a form of the auxiliary *be* + *-ing*). This is called the **continuous aspect**.

> I *am* still *studying* French.
> He *was living* in St. Paul all that year.
> Javier *is helping out* with the children this week.
> Sarina and Sindar *were looking* for a new apartment at the time.

– the fact that an action has been completed (using a form of the auxiliary *have* + a past participle, usually *-ed*). This is called the **perfect aspect**.

> I *have been* a teacher for four years.
> He *had lived* in Lincoln for a year before coming to Omaha.
> Javier *has helped out* before.
> Sarina and Sindar *had found* their apartment by then.

The two aspects of the verb can be joined so that we can talk about the duration and the completion of an action in the same verb phrase. See pp. 39–69 for more on tense and aspect.

> I *have been studying* French for four years.
> I *had been living* in Topeka for four years when I met him.
> Paula *has been helping* us this week.

Present and past simple tenses

Simple tenses show moments in time, states that do not depend on time, and habitual or repetitive actions.

> It **tastes** good.
> Julie **keeps** a diary.
> Adrian **went** home at midnight.
> She **heard** a strange noise in the night.
> Raja usually **walks** to school.

The **present simple** and the **past simple tenses** of regular verbs are formed by using the base form of the verb. See pp. 47–48 and 55–56.

Continuous forms

Continuous forms show that something lasted or continued over a period of time.

> It **is raining** hard this morning.
> It **was raining** when we came out of school yesterday.
> I'm **having** dinner. Can I call you back?
> He **was listening** to the radio when he heard the news.

The **present continuous** and the **past continuous** are formed from either the present or the past tense of the verb **be** + the **present participle** (or -ing form) of the main verb. See pp. 49–50 and 57–58.

Perfect forms

The present perfect shows that an action is completed but that it still has some importance in the present time.

> Ken **has walked** all the way from the train station. (...and he's tired.)
> He **has** never **visited** me. (...and I'm feeling neglected.)
> She **has missed** the train. (That's why she's not here.)

With verbs that indicate states rather than actions, the present perfect shows that a state or condition began in the past and continues in the present.

> Ken **has felt** ill all morning. (...he still feels ill.)
> He **has** never **believed** me. (...and he doesn't believe me now.)
> She **has missed** him terribly since he left. (...she still misses him.)

The **past perfect** is used to talk about something that happened at a time before a particular time in the past.

> I **had** never **been** climbing before our vacation last year.
> She was late because she **had missed** her train.

The **present perfect** and the **past perfect** are formed using either the present or the past tense of the verb **have** + **the past participle** of the main verb. See pp. 51–52 and 59–60.

Perfect continuous forms

Perfect continuous forms show duration, completion, and importance.

> I **have been working** hard in the garden all day.
> My mother **has been helping** me.
> I **had been working** in Calgary that summer.
> Some of us **had been waiting** for two hours when the doctor appeared.

The **present perfect continuous** and the **past perfect continuous** are formed using either the present or past tense of the verb **have** + **the past participle** of **be** + **the present participle** of the main verb. See p. 53–54 and 61–62.

Other verb forms

Other verb combinations are used for positive or negative statements, or to express degrees of time and probability.

> **Do** you **like** espresso coffee?
> I **don't like** fried food.
> **Could** I **have** a Coke, please?
> We **will be** in Elkhart within two hours.
> They **will** probably **meet** us at the airport.

Types of main verb

Verbs of action

Most verbs describe an action, for example, *walking*, *running*, or *reading*.

> Juan **is running** for the train.
> Sophie **has** just **bought** a new camera.
> She **is putting on** an exhibition of her photographs.
> Rabindrinath **has seen** the movie already.

- Action verbs can be expressed in all forms and tenses.

Verbs of state

Some verbs are used to talk about states of being or states of mind.

These include:

- verbs relating to the senses, e.g., *feel, hear, see, smell, taste*

- verbs relating to emotions, e.g., *adore, fear, hate, like, love, want, wish*

- verbs relating to mental activity, e.g., *agree, believe, expect, forget, mean*

- verbs relating to possession, e.g., *belong, own, possess*

> I **feel** unhappy.
> I **hate** arguments.
> These flowers **smell** gorgeous.
> Roberto **wishes** he **hadn't agreed** to the plan.
> We **mean** you no harm.
> That car **belonged** to us once.

- Verbs of state are not usually used in continuous forms. When they are used in continuous forms, they change their meaning.

> I'm just **feeling** to see if the bone is broken.
> We **were tasting** some interesting New Mexico wines.
> Naomi **is expecting** a baby.

There are some uses of the verb **be** that allow you to choose between a state or an action meaning. The word used as the complement makes an important difference.

Mark **is being** silly	**but not** ~~Mark is being tall~~.
Oscar **is being** nasty	**but not** ~~Oscar is being intelligent~~.

The verb **seem** has a limited number of adjectives that can be used as its complement.

Simon seems **happy**	**but not** ~~Simon seems tall~~.

The forms of main verbs

English verbs have up to five different forms. These are:

1   the base form   *pull*
2   the 3rd person singular, present simple   *pulls*
3   the past simple   *pulled*
4   the past participle   *pulled*
5   the present participle   *pulling*

- Regular verbs are all formed in the same way, by adding endings onto the **base form** (form 1). These endings indicate either the time of action or the person performing the action. Most verbs are regular.

- Irregular verbs have different forms, particularly forms 3 and 4. See pp. 13–15 for a list of irregular verbs and their inflections.

Form 1: In the **present simple** tense, all forms are the same as the **base form**, except one.

Form 2: When the **present simple** has a 3rd person singular subject, the verb is formed from the **base form** + **-s**.

Form 3: The **past simple** is formed from the **base form** + **-ed**.

Form 4: The **past participle** is formed from the **base form** + **-ed**.

Form 5: The **present participle** is formed from the **base form** + **-ing**.

A special variation of the base form is the **to infinitive**. There are a number of uses of a verb where both the words **to** + the **base form** must be present.

> The base form is sometimes called the *'bare infinitive'*.

As mentioned above, the 3rd person singular is formed from the **base form** + **-s**. Below are the exceptions to the rule:

–   verbs ending in **-o**, **-s**, **-ch**, **-sh**, **-ss**, **-x**, **-z** or **-zz**: add **-es** to make the 3rd person singular, e.g..

torpedo	he torpedo**es**	miss	he miss**es**
catch	he catch**es**	box	he box**es**
focus	he focus**es**	buzz	it buzz**es**
push	he push**es**		

– verbs ending in **-y** after a consonant: change -y to -i and add **-es**, e.g..

carry	he carr**ies**
fly	he fl**ies**
worry	he worr**ies**

As mentioned above, you form the past simple tense and past participle of regular verbs from the **base form** + **-ed**. However, you do not form the past simple tense and past participle of irregular verbs with **-ed**. See pp. 13–15 for a list of irregular verbs and their inflections.

| bent | spent | did |
| gone | done | fallen |

As mentioned above, the present participle is made up of the **base form** + **-ing**. There are some exceptions to the rule:

Verbs of one syllable that contain a short final vowel in front of a final consonant double the consonant before **-ing**, e.g.

sob	sobbing	stop	stopping
bid	bidding	get	getting
flog	flogging	put	putting
run	running		

Note that the consonants **h**, **j**, **k**, **q**, **v**, **w**, **x**, and **y** are not doubled before **-ing**, e.g.

| box | boxing | claw | clawing |
| buy | buying | | |

Verbs that end in a double consonant retain this when forming the present participle.

add	adding
toss	tossing

If the verb has two syllables, the consonant at the end should be doubled, but only if the emphasis is on the second syllable.

forget	forgetting
occur	occurring
cancel	canceling
travel	traveling

Many English verbs end with a silent **-e**. When you add the present participle **-ing** to these verbs, you drop the **-e**.

hope	hoping
desire	desiring
guide	guiding

A few verbs have variant endings in **-ing** and **-eing**, e.g.

aging	ageing
gluing	glueing

However, note that **dying** and **dyeing** are not variant endings but the present participles of the verbs **die** and **dye** which have different meanings.

You add a **k** to verbs that end in **-c** before adding **-ing** in order to preserve the hard sound.

mimic	mimicking
panic	panicking
picnic	picnicking

Tense

Time reference

Verb forms help us make time reference through their **tense**. Tense shows whether an action or a state took place in the past or takes place in the present. There are two **simple tenses**: **present simple** and **past simple**.

> Jessica **works** in the post office. (present simple)
> Laurence **worked** in the post office over the Christmas holidays. (past simple)

Simple tenses

The present and past simple tenses consist of a single word.

There is a **present simple** tense

> I **like**   I **live**
> you **like**   you **live**
> he **likes**   he **lives**

and a **past simple** tense.

> I **liked**   I **lived**
> you **liked**   you **lived**
> he **liked**   he **lived**

The simple tenses of regular verbs

The **present tense** is the same as the **base form** of the verb, except that an -*s* is added to the verb when it has a noun or *he*, *she*, or *it* as a subject. This is called the 3rd person singular form.

> *he/she/it* like**s**
> *he/she/it* live**s**

The **past tense** of a regular verb is made from the **base form** of the verb with -*ed* (or -*d* if the verb already ends in -*e*) added. The spelling is the same for all persons.

> *I* **liked**   *I* **lived**
> *you* **liked**   *you* **lived**
> *he* **liked**   *he* **lived**

The simple tenses of irregular verbs

Most irregular verbs make the **present tense** from the **base form** of the verb just as regular verbs do.

> **Present**
> *I* **find**   *I* **go**
> *you* **find**   *you* **go**
> *he/she/it* **finds** *he/she/it* **goes**

- Irregular verbs make the **past tense** in a number of different ways. Sometimes the past tense is a completely different word. See pp. 13–15 for more on irregular verbs.

> **Past**
> *I* **found**   *I* **went**
> *you* **found**   *you* **went**
> *he/she/it* **found** *he/she/it* **went**

Aspect

When we use a verb, we often need to be able to talk about the fact that the action was continuous, or that it was completed. **Aspect** describes the way we think of verbal actions.

The **continuous aspect** is formed by using the appropriate form of the auxiliary *be* together with the *-ing* form (**present participle**) of the main verb.

We use **continuous aspect** to show that an action:

– is happening at the time of speaking.

> I*'m having* dinner at the moment. Can I call you back?
> I know what you *are doing*!
> Look! Someone*'s walking* around in our garden!

– was happening throughout the time that you are talking about.

> I *was having* dinner when he called.
> I *was waiting* for her when she came out of the classroom.
> We *were driving* home when we saw the accident.

– will be happening at the time that you are talking about.

> We*'re going* to Tulsa for the holidays next year.
> They*'re coming* to us for Christmas this year.

The **perfect aspect** is formed by using the appropriate form of the auxiliary *have* together with the *-ed* form (**past participle**) of the main verb.

We use **perfect aspect** to show that an action:

- is complete at the time of speaking.

  I**'ve finished** the book. It was fantastic.
  We**'ve enjoyed** having you all to stay.
  Jolene **has borrowed** the book, so I can't check now, I'm afraid.

- was complete at the time you are referring to.

  I **had forgotten** my promise to Aunt Sissy.
  Sharon **had lost** her key, so she had to wait outside.
  Sue **had seen** the film three times already, but she didn't mind.

> It is possible to have a form that shows both aspects:
> continuous and perfect.
>
> Peter **has been talking** about you a lot recently.

Continuous and perfect forms

These forms are a combination of present or past **tense** (shown through an auxiliary verb) with continuous or perfect **aspect**. See also pp. 41–42.

> I'**m doing** my homework at the moment, so I can't come out.
> Marcel **has seen** the camera that he wants.
>
> She **was listening** to the radio in the kitchen.
> Sandra **had invited** all her friends.

- The tense of the auxiliary verb shows whether the form is in the **present** tense,

> I'**m having** dinner at the moment; I'll call you back.
> We'**ve had** a fantastic stay; thank you.

or the **past** tense.

> We **were dancing** around the living room and singing along.
> Mom **had gone out** and left us some snacks.

The choice of the **auxiliary** and the **participle** shows what aspect the verb has.

- If it is the auxiliary **be** and the **-ing** participle (the present participle), the aspect is **continuous**.

> My brother **is having** a party tomorrow.
> The kids **were running** wild when we got home.

- If it is the auxiliary **have** and the **-ed** participle (the past participle) the aspect is **perfect**.

> Jill **has walked** more than 500 miles for charity.
> Someone **had tied up** the dog to keep it from wandering off.

These are the main continuous and perfect forms:

present continuous
= present of **be** + **-ing** participle.

> *Kerry **is waiting** until Jessica gets here.*

past continuous
= past of **be** + **-ing** participle.

> *Maria **was watching** TV when Josh called.*

present perfect
= present of **have** + **-ed** participle.

> *Sam **has purchased** a few things that he likes.*
> *We**'ve borrowed** some better equipment.*

past perfect
= past of **have** + **-ed** participle.

> *She **had** really **believed** their story!*
> *Rory **had had** enough of their stupid questions.*

It is possible to combine both the continuous and perfect forms, using **two auxiliary verbs** and a **main verb**. This produces the following combinations:

present perfect continuous
= present of **have** + past participle of **be** + **-ing** participle.

> *For the past two months, Zoe **has been visiting** us once a week.*
> *We**'ve been trying** to finish that job since Easter.*

past perfect continuous
= past of **have** + past participle of **be** + **-ing** participle.

> *Vicky **had been hoping** for better news.*
> *I **had been traveling all day**, so I was exhausted.*

The modal auxiliaries can be used with continuous and perfect forms.

> *She **might be babysitting** for us on Friday.*
> *We **would be sitting** here for hours if I told you everything.*
> *I **may have eaten** something that disagreed with me.*
> *I expect Nayeema **will have bought** something for supper.*

They come in first position in the verb phrase, so they are followed by:

–   the subject and the rest of the verb in questions.

> ***Will you be going** shopping after work?*

–   the negative **not** and the rest of the verb in negative statements.

> *Marcus **may not have been** entirely truthful.*

–   the subject, the negative **not**, and the rest of the verb in negative questions.

> ***Will you not be pushing** for that to be changed?*

If the contracted negative form of the modal is used, then it comes before the subject and the rest of the verb.

> ***Won't** he **be calling** on us this evening?*

> Modals are not used with the supporting auxiliary verb **do**.

Short responses

In short responses, you usually use only one of the auxiliary verbs.
If it is a simple tense, you use the supporting auxiliary **do**
(see pp. 158–163).

> **Do** you **like** avocados? – Yes, I **do**.

If one of the forms of **be** or **have** is the first verb in the verb phrase,
then you use that as the response form.

> **Has** Claire been here yet? – Yes, she **has**.
> **Was** Nadia asking for help? – Yes, she **was**.

If a **modal** verb is first in the verb phrase, some speakers prefer to use
the modal and the auxiliary form together as the response form.

> Do you think he **might have left** the box somewhere? –
>   Yes, he **might** or Yes, he **might have**.
> So Laurence **could be coming** with us then –
>   Yes, he **could** or Yes, he **could be**.

The present

There are four ways of expressing the present in English: the present simple, the present continuous, the present perfect, and the present perfect continuous. You use the present forms to refer to a time that includes the present.

The present simple tense

Typical forms of this tense are:

> I **know** her.
> He **knows** her.

> I **don't know** her.
> He **doesn't know** her.

> **Do** you **know** her?
> **Does** she **know** him?

We use the present simple tense to:

- talk about habits, likes and dislikes, and things that happen regularly.

> I **like** coffee for breakfast but everyone else in my family
>   **prefers** tea.
> I **don't like** sugar in my coffee.
> What **does** Jamie **usually have** for breakfast?
> They **often go** to the movies **on Saturdays**.
> I **don't usually watch** TV.

(When we talk about habits, we often add adverbs such as *often*, *always*, *usually*, *sometimes*, or *never*, or adverbial phrases such as *on Sundays* or *in the summer*.)

- make statements of fact that are scientific truths or that are about a permanent state.

> The sun **rises** in the east.
> Birds **fly** south in the winter.
> We **live** in Scottsdale.

- make statements that indicate the speaker's opinions or beliefs.

> I **think** he's a very good teacher.
> I **don't agree** with that at all.

- tell a story or describe an action vividly, for dramatic narrative.

> He **walks** slowly to the checkout and **puts** his bag on the counter.
> As the cashier **opens** the register he **draws** a gun ...

- give a commentary on a sports event or public function.

> ... but Nadal **sees** it. He **runs** up to the net and **smashes** the ball.

We can also use the present simple for planned future actions with a time adverb, for example to talk about travel plans and timetables. See pp. 63–69 for more about future reference.

> The flight **leaves** at 10:40 a.m. and **arrives** at 3:30 p.m.

We use the present simple in conditional sentences about real possibilities that affect the future.

> If I **lend** you my notes, I won't be able to review tonight.

The present continuous

Typical forms are:

> I *am winning*.
> He *is winning*.
>
> **Am** I **winning**?
> **Is** she **winning**?
>
> I *am not winning*.
> He *is not winning*.
>
> **Aren't** I **winning**?
> **Isn't** she **winning**?
>
> **Am** I **not winning**?
> **Is** she **not winning**?

Some main verbs are not normally used in the continuous in standard or formal English, although they may be used this way in other varieties of English. These are generally verbs about states rather than actions.

> I *am winning*.   **but not** ~~I am liking it~~.
> I *am not winning*. **but not** ~~I am not liking it~~.

We use the present continuous to talk about:

– things that are happening now, at the time when we are talking.

> Mom**'s mowing** the lawn, and I**'m doing** my homework,
>   but Kaitlin **isn't doing** anything.
> The children aren't asleep; they**'re goofing off**.
> Come on; you**'re not trying**.

- a temporary activity, even if it is not happening at the time when we are talking.

    I'm studying German in college.
    I'm thinking of getting a new car.

- a temporary situation in contrast to a permanent situation.

    I'm living in Midland at the moment.
    Frieda is working in the stables over the holidays.

- a changing state or situation.

    My headache is getting better.
    The daylight is slowly fading.

- the circumstances under which something is generally done.

    I have to wear glasses when I'm driving.

- arrangements for future events along with a time adverb or phrase like *tomorrow*, *next week*, or *later*. See pp. 62–68 for more on the future.

    I am flying to New York next week.

We also use it to express annoyance at a repeated action. In this case, one of the following adverbs is used with the verb: *always, forever, constantly, continually*.

    She's always complaining about something.
    He's forever laughing and making silly comments.

When you give a short answer to a question, it is normal to repeat the auxiliary, but not the main verb.

    Are you waiting for someone? – Yes, I am.
    Is Hamish working in the library? – No, he isn't.

The present perfect

You use the present perfect to talk about the present effects of something which happened at a time in the past.

Typical forms are:

> I **have finished**.
> He **has found** them.
> They**'ve finished**.
> They**'ve found** her.
> Listen! I**'ve heard** some great news; Jim**'s won**!
> They**'ve bought** a brand new car.
> You**'ve got** a lot of nerve!

> **Have** they **finished**? – No, they **haven't**.
> **Has** Mary **arrived** yet? – No, she **hasn't**.

> I **have** not **finished**.
> He **has** not **finished**.
> Ranee **hasn't found** her bracelet yet.
> They **haven't seen** her.

The contracted forms are:

> has = **'s**   have = **'ve**
> has not = **hasn't**   have not = **haven't**

The present perfect is used to talk about events that relate to the present but that happened in the past. It is also used to talk about an action that started in the past, without mentioning a specific time.

> Her daughter **has had** an accident.
> We **have seen** the Eiffel Tower and the Arc de Triomphe.

If the present perfect occurs more than once in a sentence, the second instance of **have** can be left out.

> They **have bought** their tickets and **chosen** their seats.

- We can use *just* if we want to show that the action has very recently been completed.

> He **has just finished** his homework.

If the event did not take place you can use *never*. If you want to find out whether it took place or not, you can use *ever*.

> **Have** you **ever been** to Greece?
> I'**ve never done** anything like this before.

- If we want to indicate a moment in time or a period of time, we can use expressions such as *recently*, *lately*, *this morning*, *today*, or *this week* with the present perfect.

> I **haven't been** to the movies **recently**.

- In questions and negative sentences, the present perfect can be used with *yet*, meaning "at the time of speaking". In positive sentences, use *already*.

> **Haven't** you **finished yet**?
> **Have** you **bought** the tickets **yet**?
> I'**ve already seen** that movie.

The present perfect is often used to answer the question *How long...?* together with *for* to talk about a period of time, or *since* to talk about duration from a point in time.

> I **have lived** in Edmonton **for** fifteen years.
> We'**ve had** this car **since** 2008.

The present perfect continuous

You use the present perfect continuous to talk about the present effects of something that started in the past.

Typical forms are:

> I **have been waiting**.
> I'**ve been waiting**.
> She **has been waiting**.
> She'**s been waiting**.

> **Have** I **been snoring**?
> **Has** he **been waiting**?
> **Have** you **been waiting** long?

> I **have** not **been waiting**.
> She **has** not **been waiting**.

We use the present perfect continuous to talk about:

— actions and states that began in the past and are still continuing at the time of speaking.

> I **have been holding** this ladder for ages. When are you going to come down?

— actions and states that began in the past and have just finished.

> Thank goodness you're here! I'**ve been waiting** for hours.

— repeated actions.

> I'**ve been getting** this magazine every week for a year.

There is sometimes little difference between the meaning of the present perfect and the meaning of the present perfect continuous when they are used for long-term actions.

> **I have been working** here for three years.
> **I have worked** here for three years.

We usually choose the continuous form for more temporary actions or states,

> **I have been living** in Seattle since I left school.

and the present perfect form for more permanent ones.

> **I have lived** in Seattle since I was born.

- We cannot use this form with verbs such as *be*, *know*, and *like*, which are not used in the continuous.

We can use *for* and *since* with the continuous form in the same way as with the present perfect. See also pp. 49–50 and pp. 57–58 for more about continuous uses of the verb.

> **I have been studying** English for three years.
> **I have studied** English for three years.

> **I have been living** in Portland since I left school.
> **I have lived** in Portland since I was born.

The past

There are four ways of talking about the past in English: the past simple, the past continuous, the past perfect, and the past perfect continuous. You use the past tenses to refer to past time and to express politeness.

The past simple tense

You use the past simple tense for events which happened in the past.

Typical forms of this tense are:

> I **met** her.
> She **met** him.
> **Did** you **meet** her?
> I **didn't meet** her.
> I **went** there.
> **Did** you **go** there?
> She **went** there.
> She **didn't go** there.

We use the past simple tense to talk about:

- single actions in the past.

> He **locked** the door and **left** the house.
> I **went** out and **brought** the cat back in again.

- habitual actions in the past, often with *always*, *never*, or *often*.

> In those days I **always went** to Juliano's for lunch.
> I **bicycled** in **every day** and that soon **made** me fit.
> I **often visited** Boston on business when I was in publishing.

- past actions where a definite time is mentioned. It is often used with a time expression such as *ago* or *last month*, when the action is seen as finished.

> **Some time ago** now, I **went** to Nicaragua for a month.
> **Once upon a time** there **was** a king in a faraway land.
> I **saw** Roger **a little while back**.
> I **bought** the microwave **a year ago**.

- points where the main action is broken. The rest of the sentence uses the past continuous to describe the past activity or action.

> I was clearing out the garage when a car **came** down the drive.
> We were leaving the house when the phone **rang**.

• The past simple tense can also make an offer sound more polite.

> **Did** you **want** to see me now?
> **rather than** **Do** you **want** to see me now?

The past continuous

Typical forms are:

I **was winning**.   **but not** ~~I was liking it~~.
She **was winning**.
They **were winning**.

Was I **winning**?
Was she **winning**?
Were you **winning**?

I **was not winning**   **but not** ~~I was not liking it~~.
We **were not winning**.
They **weren't winning**.

Some main verbs are not normally used in the continuous in standard English, although they may be used this way in some varieties of English. These are generally verbs about states rather than feelings. We use the past continuous in these ways:

– with a time expression, such as *at 6 p.m. yesterday*, to talk about an action that began before that time and finished after it. The exact length of time the action took is not important.

   *What **were you doing** at eight o'clock last night? –*
   *I **was standing** at the bus stop.*

– to talk about an interrupted action. Note that we use the past simple tense to talk about the event that interrupts the action.

   *We **were** all **sitting** in our places when the bell **rang**.*

– to talk about a short action that happened while a longer one was already taking place.

   *While I **was waiting** for the bus I **dropped** my purse.*

- to describe a scene in the past, especially in a story.

  > *It was a dreadful morning. The snow **was still falling**, the wind **was blowing**, and the cars **were skidding** on the icy roads.*

- The past continuous can also make a request sound more polite.

  > *I **was wondering** if you could help me.*
  > **rather than** *I **wonder** if you can help me.*

The past perfect

You use the past perfect when you are already talking about a point in the past, and you then want to talk about something that happened at an earlier time.

Typical forms are:

> I **had forgotten** my bag.
> She **had forgotten** her bag.
> I **had finished**.
> She **had found** them.
> She**'d gone**.
> They**'d found** her.

> **Had** I **forgotten** my bag?
> **Had** it **gone**?
> **Had** Mary **arrived** before Peter told you? – No, she **hadn't**.

> I **had** not **forgotten** my bag.
> He **had forgotten** his bag.
> I **had** not **finished**.
> It **had** not **worked**.
> I **hadn't realized** how serious the problem was.
> They **hadn't seen** her.

The contracted forms are:

> had = **'d**   had not = **hadn't**

The past perfect goes one step further back into the past than the present perfect.

> **Had** you ever **seen** her before then? – No, I **hadn't**.

The past perfect is used to talk about:

- an action that took place in the past before something else took place.

    *She **had just made** some coffee when I arrived.*

- an action or state that began before another action in the past and continued up to the time of the second action and perhaps even beyond that time.

    *Ashraf **had** already **known** my brother **for two years** when I met him.*

- It is often used in the main clause of a complex sentence, to set the scene for a past event.

    *I **had seen** him several times before Jane finally introduced us.*

- It is often used with a time expression such as *always* or *for several days*.

    *We **had always wanted** to visit Canada, so last year we decided to go.*

The past perfect continuous

You use the past perfect continuous when you are already talking about the past and you want to talk about something that had started at an earlier time and was still continuing.

Typical forms are:

> I **had been waiting**.
> I**'d been waiting**.
> She **had been waiting**.
> She**'d been waiting**.

> **Had I been talking in my sleep**? *What had I said?*
> **Had he been waiting** *long?*
> **Had you been expecting** *to meet Maia at the bus station?*

> I **had not been waiting**.
> She **had not been waiting**.
> They **hadn't been looking** *very carefully.*

- The past perfect continuous is used to talk about an action which began before another action in the past and either:

- continued up to the time of the second action,

> I **hadn't been waiting** *long when a bus came up beside me.*

- or was completed before the second action happened.

> I **had been studying** *and decided to take a stroll to clear my mind.*
> We **had been cleaning** *the car for hours, so we stopped and had a drink.*

- The past perfect continuous is often used in the main clause of a complex sentence, to set the scene for an event.

> I **had been driving** for about an hour when I **heard** a noise in the engine.

* The past perfect continuous is often used to talk about a repeated action.

> She **had been trying** to telephone her mother all day.

> Remember that you cannot use the past perfect continuous with verbs such as *like*, which are not used in the continuous. See p. 49.

Future reference

Verb forms

English has no future tense as such. However, several forms, especially the **modal** verbs *will* and *shall* (see pp. 216–218), can be used to make future reference. These forms are summarized as follows:

1 *Will/shall* + the **base form** makes the most direct form of future reference. The other modal verbs that express possibility make a more indirect reference to future time.
> It **will take** *several years to finish*.
> *Jean* **will look after** *the dogs while we're away*.
> *I'll simply* **tell** *her to mind her own business*.
> *We* **shall see**.

2 *Be going to* + the **base form** is used to express intention and make predictions. See pp. 130–131.
> *He failed his exam last year; this year he* **is going to work** *harder*.
> *You'd better take the laundry in; it* **is going to rain**.

3 The **present continuous** is used to talk about plans and arrangements in the future with a time adverb.
> *Sarah and Harriet* **are meeting at ten o'clock** *on* **Tuesday**.
> *I* **am flying** *to Georgia* **on Friday**.

4 The **present simple** is used with a time adverb to talk about future plans which are part of a timetable or previous arrangement. See pp. 47–48
> *The main feature* **starts at 2:45 p.m.**
> *We* **leave at 4 p.m. tomorrow**.

5 The **future perfect** (*will have* + the **past participle**) is used with a time adverb to talk about an action that will be finished at the time in the future that you are referring to. See p. 68.
> *I was hoping to meet Jorge, but by the time I arrive he* **will have gone** *home*.

6 *be about to* + the **base form** is used to talk about the very near future. See p. 68.

> *I'm sorry I can't stop and chat; I**'m about to leave** for work.*

7 The **future continuous** (*will be* + the **present participle**) is used to talk about future action in progress. See p. 69.

> *What **will** you **be doing** on Saturday morning? Oh, I'll be shopping as usual.*

8 *Be to* + the **base form** is used to talk about formal plans, especially in journalism. See p. 69 and p. 124.

> *The President **is to attend** an EU–Russia summit tomorrow.*

1 will/shall

The modal verbs *will* or *shall* followed by the **base form** of a main verb are used to express future reference.

I **shall come**. or	We **shall come**. or
I **will come**.	We **will come**.
You **will come**.	You **will come**.
She/he/it **will come**.	They **will come**.

• *Will* is normally used with all persons of the verb. Some older speakers, or people speaking in formal contexts, prefer to use *shall* in the 1st person singular and plural.

• The contracted form is *'ll* for both verbs, so there is no difference in informal speech.

> *I'll probably be late, but I expect they'll be on time.*

The contracted negative forms are **won't** and **shan't**, but **shan't** is almost never heard in American English.

> *We **won't come**.*
> *We **shan't come**.*

- If there are two verbs in the sentence, it is normal not to repeat the modal form before the second one.
    *I **won't go** and see him or **speak** to him for six months.*

We use **will** (or **shall**) for future reference in the following ways (see also pp. 216–217).

– To talk about future facts.
    *I **won't see** Murray next week.*
    *I'll **be** on the plane this time tomorrow.*

– To make promises or reassurances.
    *I'll **be** home in time for dinner.*
    *This **won't happen** again, I can assure you.*

– To announce a decision that the speaker has just made.
    *I'll **have** the pizza and a side salad, please.*
    *Right, I'll **ask** him, and see what he says.*

– To express a decision not to do something, using **won't**.
    *I **won't go** there again. The service was terrible.*

– To express refusal.
    *I **won't put up with** any more of this silly behavior.*
    *I've tried to persuade her but she **won't come**.*

– To talk about an event in the future, possibly in the distant future. A time clause may be used.
    *People **will be** amazed when they hear about this in years to come.*

– To refer to inevitable actions or events that will take place in the future.
    *Christmas is over, but it **will come** again next year.*

– To express an opinion about a future event after verbs such as *believe, expect, hope, know,* and *think*.

*I **expect** he'll be home soon.*
*I **hope** you'll be very happy in your new home.*

– To express a real possibility in conditional sentences.
   *If you phone after six I'll **tell** you all about it.*

2 be going to

Future reference can be made with **be** + **going to** + the **base form** of a main verb. See also pp. 130–131.

   *I **am going to wait**.*
   *He **is going to wait**.*
   *I **am not going to wait**.*
   *He **is not going to wait**.*
   ***Is** he **going to wait**?*
   ***Are** they **going to wait**?*

Be going to is used in the following ways.

– To express intention about the future.
   *Mary **isn't going** to study art; she**'s going** to be a nurse.*

– To talk about things that have already been decided.
   *Is Jim **going to leave** his job? – Yes, **he is**.*
   *Where's Mary? She said she **was going to come** early.*

– To make a prediction about the future, often the very near future, based on something in the present.
   *Watch the milk! It **is going to boil** over!*
   *Sally never does any work; she **is going to fail** her exams.*

If the past tense of **be** is used, a past intention or prediction can be expressed.

   *Judy **was going to meet** me, but she was ill and couldn't come.*
   *She **was** obviously **going to get** sore feet with those new shoes.*

Note this difference:
Be going to is usually used for future events where the speaker expresses his or her intention.
Will is used to express decisions made at the moment of speaking.
I'm going to go to the movies on Friday; would you like to come? Yes, I'll go if Chris goes.

3 Present continuous

This is made with the appropriate form of *be* + the **present participle** of a main verb. The present continuous is used to talk about plans for the future, or specific arrangements that people have made for future events.

> *The school **is having** a bake sale next week; I**'m organizing** it.*

It is often used in questions about future arrangements.

> *What **are you doing** on Saturday? – I**'m going** to a football game with Peter.*
> *When **are you leaving**? – At the end of term.*

If there are two or more verbs in the sentence, it is normal not to repeat the auxiliary before the second and subsequent ones.

> *We **are meeting** at 12:30 p.m., **having** a quick lunch, and **starting** work at 1:15.*

4 Present simple

The present simple is also used to talk about events that form part of a timetable or program.

> *The flight **leaves** Albuquerque at 10:10 a.m. and **arrives** in Baltimore at 3:20 p.m.*
> *These are the arrangements for Friday: the Mayor **arrives** at 7:30 p.m. and the meeting **starts** at 7:45 p.m.*

5 The future perfect

This is made with **will have** + the **past participle** of a main verb. This form is used to talk about an action that will be complete at a time in the future that you are talking about. It is often used with verbs relating to finishing or completing.

The contracted positive form is **'ll have** or **will've**.

> *Can you come over next Saturday? – Yes, I'll **have finished** my exams by then.*
> *Dad **will've made** dinner by the time we get back.*

The contracted negative is **won't have**.

> *The essay is due on Tuesday, but I **won't have completed** it by then.*

In questions, the subject comes after **will**. The short answer to a question is **will** without the past participle.

> **Will** you **have finished** dinner by then? – Yes, **we will**.

6 be about to

The appropriate form of **be** + **about to** + the **base form** of a main verb is used to talk about events in the very near future.

> *Turn off the stove – the soup **is about to boil** over.*
> *Come on! The movie's **about to start**!*

It is sometimes used with **just** to give even more immediacy.

> *Quick, jump in! The train **is (just) about to leave**.*

Be about to can also be used in the **past** to suggest that someone was *on the verge of* carrying out an action when it was interrupted. In this case it is usually followed by **when**.

> *They **were (just) about to go** to bed **when** the phone rang.*

7 The future continuous

This is made with **will** + **be** + the **present participle** of a main verb.
Will be forms negatives, contractions, questions, and short answers in the usual way.

The future continuous is used in an informal way to suggest that something is about to happen or will happen at some time that is not clear or precise.

> I'**ll be seeing** you.
> We'**ll be getting** in touch with you.
> They'**ll be wanting** us to clean our own classrooms next!
> We **won't be seeing** Uncle John while we are in Arizona.

It is also used to talk about an activity that will already be happening at a particular time in the future.

> **Will** you **be working** here next week?
> No, I won't. I'**ll be starting** my new job.
> Just think! This time next week, we **will be flying** to Sydney.

8 be to

The appropriate form of **be** + **to** + the **base form** of a main verb is used mainly in fairly formal English to talk about plans, arrangements, and instructions. It indicates that what will happen is part of an expected process, and is often found in journalistic texts.

> Foreign ministers of the NATO countries **are to meet** in
>   Brussels next week.
> The President has left for Geneva, where he **is to attend** the
>   meeting.

Active and Passive

Active sentences

In the following example, the verb is **active**.

> *The post office delivers thousands of letters every day.*

The subject of an active sentence is also the person or thing that carries out the action. We use the active when the subject of the verb is the doer of the action. The active is used in most English speech and writing, because we usually want to inform our listener or our reader who or what carried out the action of the verb.

> *He hid the money under the bed.*
> *The car knocked over a pedestrian.*
> *I'm sending the book by express mail.*

Passive sentences

In the following example, the verb is in the **passive**.

> *Thousands of letters are delivered every day.*

The subject in a passive sentence is not the person or thing that does the action of the verb; it is the person or thing that is acted on by the verb.

> *The injured man was helped by a passer-by.*
> *The man was being questioned by the police.*
> *The patient was operated on by a team of five surgeons.*

The passive is made with the appropriate form of **be** + the **past participle** of the main verb.

- We use the passive to direct our listener's or reader's attention to the important part of our message. For instance, in the first example of this section we do not need to know who delivers the letters, so all mention of the post office is left out.

- We can use the passive when we do not know who carries out the action expressed by the verb, or when it is not important that we should know. It is sometimes much more important to know what has happened than who or what did it.

  > *The money **was hidden** under the bed.*
  > *The book **is being sent** by express mail.*
  > *An elderly man **was run over** while crossing the road.*
  > *Roger **has been given** his promotion.*
  > *The patient **was operated on**.*

The passive allows us to select the parts of a sentence that we want to draw attention to. It can be used when we want to focus on:

- the **agent**, i.e. the person who carried out the action. We show the agent with *by*.

  > *The window was broken **by some boys**.*
  > *My brother was given extra lessons **by his teacher**.*
  > *The old man was run over **by a careless driver**.*
  > *The patient was operated on **by a team of top surgeons**.*

- the **instrument**, i.e. what was used to make the action happen. We show the instrument with *by* or *with*.

  > *The sorting is done **by machine**.*
  > *The safe was blown open **with dynamite**.*
  > *The old man was knocked over **by a bus**.*
  > *I was showered **with presents** on my eighteenth birthday.*

– the **means**, i.e., what caused the action to happen. We show the means with *by* or *with*.

> The window was shattered **by the explosion**.
> He was exhausted **with the strain of caring for his elderly parents**.
> Spelling errors are marked **with an X in the margin**.
> He was taken to the hospital **by ambulance**.

The subject of a passive verb

In a passive sentence, the word that would normally be the object is in the position of the subject. When a verb has two objects, either the indirect object or the direct object of the active verb may become the subject of the passive verb.

> **I've been offered** a scholarship at Princeton.
> **We were given** a second chance.

If the indirect object is mentioned after the passive verb, the sentence must use *to*.

> The building **has been sold to** property developers.
> The medal **is awarded to** students who have shown academic excellence.

Some verbs that are often used this way are: *give, offer, promise, sell,* and *tell*.

Form of the passive

Passive verbs are made from a form of **be** + the **past participle** of a main verb. In the passive, the form of the auxiliary verb **be** indicates the tense. See also p. 124.

> They **sell** cheap computer games here.
> Cheap computer games **are sold** here.
> They **took** him to the police station for questioning.
> He **was taken** to the police station for questioning.

• Some verbs are only or mostly used in the passive, e.g. *be born*.

> My brother and I **were born** in Washington state.

The impersonal passive

This form of the passive sentence is useful when you want to report what is or was generally understood or accepted by a group of people.

> **The suitcase was found** to be empty.
> **The money is thought** to be missing.
> **The rumor is believed** to be true.

The form **it** + **passive** + **that** can be used when you do not want to mention the source of a report or rumor.

> **It is reported** that over a hundred people died in the explosion.
> **It is said** that his income is over $200 a minute.

The passive with *get*

In informal English, a type of passive is sometimes made with *get* instead of *be*.

> How did that teapot **get broken**?
> Our cat **got run over** last week.

Get is also used to form a small set of passive verbs in contexts which are not informal (that is, they are standard), e.g. *get dressed, get married, get lost*.

> Harriet **got lost** on the subway.
> When are you two **getting married**?

The causative passive with *have*

The **causative passive** expresses the idea that the subject caused or ordered someone to take the action mentioned.

> We **are having the garage door replaced**.
> She **had her hair cut short**.
> They **did not have the carpet cleaned** after all.

It has the form: **have** + **direct object** + **past participle**. More informally, the causative passive can also be formed with **get** + **direct object** + **past participle**. See also Section 2, p. 181.

> We **are getting the garage door replaced**.
> She **got her hair cut short**.
> They **did not get the carpet cleaned** after all.

Compare:
Ralph repaired his car = Ralph did the work.
*Ralph **had** his car **repaired*** or Ralph **got** his car **repaired**
   =Ralph paid someone else to do the work.

The infinitive

The infinitive is the basic form of a verb. In English, this form of the verb with the word *to* in front of it is called a **to infinitive**, and the verb form on its own is usually called **the base form** or the **bare infinitive**.

The base form

The base form of the verb is sometimes called the *bare infinitive* or the *infinitive without to*.

The **base form** is used in the following ways:

– after modal verbs. See p. 23.

> You must **stop** at the curb before you cross.
> He should **think** before he speaks.

– after *let's* (suggestion) and *let* (permission) and *make* (compulsion).

> **Let's invite** Annette over for dinner.
> **Let** the cat **go**!
> **Make** him **stop**!
> **Let** him **finish** what he was saying!

– after *feel, hear, see, watch* + an object.

> I **heard** him **run** downstairs.
> Later we **saw** them **leave** the house.

– after a **to** infinitive to which it is joined by *and*.

> I want you to sit and **listen**.
> Just wait and **see**.

– after *would rather* (see pp. 243–245) and *had better*.

> *I would rather **go** out, but I think we had better **stay** home and finish the painting.*

Verbs of perception (e.g., *see, hear, feel, smell, listen to, watch*,) may be followed either by the **base form** or by the **-*ing*** form. There is often a change of meaning.

> *We watched her **park** the car* = *We watched the whole event.*
> *We watched her **parking** the car* = *We may only have seen part of the event.*
> *I heard a cuckoo **call*** = *I heard just one call.*
> *We heard the birds **singing*** = *We heard part of the song of the birds.*

The *to* infinitive

The *to* infinitive is used:

– after an adjective of quality such as *small, tall, agreeable, pleasant, funny* that is used in combination with *too*,

> The boy was *too small to reach* the switch.
> The knife was *too dull to cut* the string.

or (*not*) + adjective of quality + *enough*.

> The boy was *not tall enough to reach* the switch.
> The knife was *not sharp enough to cut* the string.
> I was *stupid enough to go* walking in sandals.

– after adjectives of emotion such as: *angry, happy, glad, sad, sorry,* or *surprised*, to express the reason for the emotion.

> I'm *glad to see* you.
> I'm *sorry to hear* your news.

– after an adjective describing behavior such as: *good, kind, nice, silly,* or *wrong*, (sometimes + *of* + another **noun phrase**).

> It was *good of you to come*, and *kind of Jane to have sent* those flowers.
> It was *silly to go* off like that.
> It was *kind of you to call* me.

– after a **wh-** word such as: *how, what, where, whether, which, who, whom*.

> We have no idea **what to get** for Tim's birthday.
> I don't know **where to go**.
> I can't think **how to do it**.
> They were wondering **who to see** first.

–   after a noun phrase such as *a good idea, a good thing, a mistake* (sometimes + *for* + another **noun phrase**).

> It was **a mistake for Jim to buy** that motorbike.
> It was **a good idea to stop** here.

–   after an adjective such as *easy, difficult, hard, impossible* + *for* + **noun phrase**.

> It has never been **easy for David to take** exams.

–   after a verb followed by *for*, e.g., *ask, wait* + *for* + **noun phrase**.

> They **are waiting** for us **to decide**.

•   The **to** infinitive can be used to express purpose or necessity after a verb followed by a pronoun or a noun.

purpose: I brought **it to read** on the train = so that I could read it.
necessity: There is **work to do**! = work that must be done.

> Sometimes the particle **to** can be used alone, provided the meaning is clear. For example, *to* can be used in a short response when the whole verb form is used in a previous sentence or clause.
>
> > Did you **meet** Tina? No, I wanted **to**, but she was ill.
> > Are you going to **visit** the museum? Yes, we hope **to**.

The *to* infinitive and the -*ing* form

The **to** infinitive and the -**ing** form (the present participle) can each be used after certain verbs.

Verbs followed by the **to** infinitive include: *agree, arrange, attempt, choose, decide, fail, hope, learn, manage, offer, plan, seem.*

> I **agreed to help** Shona with her homework.
> The driver **attempted to remove** the flat tire.
> I **hope to see** you again at the next meeting.

Verbs followed by an **object** + the **to infinitive** include: *advise, allow, command, forbid, force, invite, order, persuade, remind, teach, tell.*

> Peter advised Ron **to call the police**.
> Esther reminded her teacher **to assign some homework**.

Verbs that can be followed *either* directly by the **to infinitive** *or* by an **object** + the **to infinitive** include: *ask, expect, help, intend, like, love, hate, mean, prefer, want, wish.*

> I certainly intended **to go** to the party.
> We really expected **Sally to pass** the exam.

Note this difference:

> I want **to have** a cat = It will be my cat.
> I want **her to have** a cat = It will be her cat.
> Dad likes **to wash** the car = Dad washes the car.
> Dad likes **John to wash** the car = John washes the car.

Verbs followed by the -**ing** form include: *avoid, be used to, delay, dislike, escape, finish, forgive, give up, go on, imagine.*

*I usually **avoid going** into town late at night.*
*Miriam **hates peeling** potatoes.*
*Have you **finished reading** that book yet?*

- Some verbs may be followed either by the **to** infinitive or by the **-ing** form with little or no change in meaning. These verbs include: *begin, start, cease, continue, intend, like, love, hate, prefer.*

    *He began **to run** around shouting.*
    *He began **running** around shouting.*

    *She likes **to swim** in the sea.*
    *She likes **swimming** in the sea.*

    *I can't bear **to see** violence.*
    *I can't bear **seeing** violence.*

- Some verbs may be followed either by the **to** infinitive or by the **-ing** form, but the meaning of the sentence changes depending on the form that is used. These verbs include: *try, forget, remember.*

    *I **remembered to switch** the lights off before we went out.*
    (= I didn't forget.)

    *I **remember switching** the lights off before we went out.*
    (= I remember that I switched them off.)

    *She **tried to talk** to him, but his secretary wouldn't put the call through.*
    (= She wanted to talk to him, but she wasn't allowed.)
    *She **tried talking** to him, but he wouldn't listen.*
    (= She tried to solve the problem by talking to him.)

Particularly after verbs such as *go* and *come*, the **to** infinitive is understood to express purpose.

> She has **gone to do** the shopping.
> They **came** here **to learn** English.

Some **set expressions** are followed by **-ing**. These include: *it's not worth*, and *it's no fun*.

> It's **no fun going** out alone.
> It's **no use phoning** him; he's gone away.
> It's **worth trying** one more time.

Verbs and affirmative, negative, interrogative, and imperative statements

Each sentence in English provides some type of information. For example, a sentence can be a statement, a question, a request, a command, a denial or a response, etc. In English the choice and order of the parts of a sentence help us express these meanings.

Most statements are in the **affirmative** or the **negative**. An important feature of these sentences is that they have a subject that comes before the verb.

> Our dog **eats** any old thing.
> Our dog **won't** just **eat** any old thing.
> The dog **has** already **been fed**.
> The dog **hasn't been fed** yet.
> We **have** already **won** several races.
> We **haven't won** any races yet.

Most questions are in the **interrogative**. An important feature of interrogative sentences is that they normally have a subject that comes after an auxiliary verb.

> **Does** your dog **eat** any old thing?
> **Has** the dog already **been fed**?
> **Hasn't** the dog **been fed** yet?
> **Have** you **won** any races yet?
> **Haven't** you **won** any races yet?

If the subject does come first it will be a special question word.

> **Who won** the race?
> **Which** team **was** it?

- We occasionally ask questions using the affirmative or the negative. We do this by using a special tone of voice.

    You're not telling me he has a new car? I don't believe it.
    It's raining again? That makes three days in a row.

Many commands are in the **imperative**. Commands in the imperative have no word that acts as a subject, though the subject is understood to be *you*. Commands in the imperative can sometimes sound rude or impatient.

    Eat up quickly. We have to go!
    Leave me alone.
    On your mark, **get set ... go!**

- We can make a **request** (which is a type of command) sound more polite by using the interrogative.

    Would you feed the dog, please?
    Would you mind shutting the door?
    Could I have that now? Thank you.

> Not all imperative sentences are orders or commands. They can be social expressions.
>
>   **Have** a nice day.
>   **Get** well soon.
>   **Help** yourselves to coffee.

There is also a **subjunctive** form that may be used when you want to talk about an improbable or unlikely situation.

    If I **were** governor, I'd spend more money on education.

Word order in affirmative statements

Affirmative sentences always contain a subject and a following verb phrase.

> *Kate is not working after all.*
> *Tim wasn't reading your diary.*
> *Hank wasn't talking about you.*
> *I'm not going on vacation this year.*

The normal word order for affirmative sentences is:

> **subject + verb phrase**
> *Kate is working.*
> *Tim was reading.*
> *Hank stared at me in surprise.*

> **subject + verb phrase + direct object**
> *Ross is writing a letter.*
> *Pam borrowed three library books.*
> *Stephen ordered vegetarian lasagna.*

> **subject + verb phrase + adverbial**
> *Dominic was eating very slowly.*
> *Lyndsey was studying in her room.*
> *Mikhail laughed nervously.*

> **subject + verb phrase + direct object + adverbial**
> *Dominic was eating his lunch very slowly.*
> *Lyndsey had been reading a book in her room.*

Certain verbs must have following objects, e.g. *see, find, prefer, take.*

> *She saw **her friend**.*
> *He found **a camera**.*
> *They took **a resort brochure**.*

Other verbs need, or can have, both a **direct** and an **indirect** object, e.g., *give, buy, offer*.

> *Laura offered* **me** *another cookie*.
> *Scott's uncle bought* **him** *a new bike*.

The word order can be either:

> **subject + verb + indirect object + direct object**
> *Kate gave* **the dog** *a bone*.
> *Stuart bought* **Marie** *a birthday present*.

or, with the addition of a word that indicates the person or animal that received something:

> **subject + verb + direct object +** *to/for* **+ indirect object**.
> *Kate gave* *a bone* **to the dog**.
> *Stuart bought* *a birthday present* **for Marie**.

Another group of verbs must be followed either by an object and an adverbial expression, or an adverbial expression on its own e.g., *put, place, stand*.

> *Richard placed* **the computer** **on the table**.
> *Diana put* **her jeans** **in the drawer**.
> *Michael stood* **in the middle of the field**.

A further type of statement has the same basic order of subject and verb as the **subject + verb phrase + direct object** example on p. 84, but with a **complement** replacing the direct object. See pp. 11–12 for more about complements.

> *Santosh seems to be* **pretty worried** *at the moment*.
> *This dessert is* **delicious**.

Word order in negative statements

In negative statements, the basic word order for subject and object is the same as in positive statements.

> *John has gone to school.*
> *John has **not** gone to school.*

The difference is that negative statements must contain ***not***, and must have as part of the verb phrase, either:

– a **primary auxiliary** verb,

> *She **had not** arrived in time for lunch.*
> *Kate **is not** working this evening.*
> *Tim **was not** reading your diary.*

– one or other of the **modal auxiliary** verbs,

> *I warn you, he **may not** want to come.*
> *Alyssa **could not** see the road clearly.*

– or a form of ***be*** used as a main verb.

> *That **is not** my book.*

The word ***not*** is added immediately after the first one of these auxiliary verbs. The main verb follows.

The word order is, therefore:

> **subject + auxiliary + *not* + main verb.**

A negative sentence may contain a modal verb and one or more auxiliaries as well.

I **may** *not* **have** *gone by the time you arrive.*
They **could** *not* **have** *seen her – they were asleep in bed.*
They **should** *not* **have been playing** *in the road.*

In this case the word order is:

subject + modal + *not* **+ primary auxiliary + main verb**.

If the verb phrase does not already contain one of these verbs, then it is necessary to add the **supporting auxiliary** verb *do*.

The present simple and the past simple tenses of main verbs take the appropriate form of *do*, and then add *not* followed by the base form of the main verb.

He runs.
He **does not** *run.*
He ran.
He **did not** *run.*
Lynn **does not** *work overtime now.*
The bus service **did not** *run on Sundays.*

The word order is therefore:

subject + *do-* **auxiliary +** *not* **+ main verb**

See pp. 158–163 for more on the supporting auxiliary *do*.

• The contracted form of *not*, which is *n't*, can be used after every auxiliary verb except *am*. This is the most common spoken form.

He **doesn't** *run.*
He **didn't** *run.*
Lynn **doesn't** *work on Sundays.*
She **hasn't** *been at work all week.*
He **isn't** *going to come after all.*
Bill went swimming but Ann **didn't** *want to.*

The full form with **not** tends to be used more in writing.

> **can + not** is written **cannot**, except when you wish to give
>   particular emphasis to not.
> She **can't** come.
> She **cannot** come.

- Other words with a negative meaning, such as **never**, **barely**, **hardly**,
  scarcely, **rarely**, do not change the order of words in a statement.

  > She **doesn't read** Vogue.
  > She **never reads** Vogue.
  > He **barely** earns enough to live on.
  > I **hardly** think that is going to put them off.

The interrogative

The interrogative is used for most types of question. It contains a verb phrase that is followed by a subject.

There are two main types of question: those that can be answered *yes* or *no*, and those that have to be answered with specific information or a sentence such as *I don't know*. Each type of question has its own special word order.

Yes/no questions

Questions that expect the answer *yes* or *no* are called **yes/no questions** or sometimes, **polar questions**.

The **interrogative** is used to form yes/no questions.

The normal sentence order for the interrogative is:

> **auxiliary verb** + **subject** + **base form** of the **main verb**.

> *Were* the dogs barking?
> *Have* you been dieting?
> *Can* Mahmoud come too?
> *Must* you go so soon?
> *Would* you like some chocolate?

When a sentence does not contain an auxiliary verb, the question is formed by placing a form of the supporting auxiliary verb *do* before the subject and following it with the **base form** of the main verb.

Does he enjoy tennis?
Do they play a lot?
Did that surprise his mom?

Note that when the main verb is *do*, you still have to add *do*, *does* or *did* before the subject.

Do they do the work themselves?
Did you do your undergraduate work at Chicago as well?

If the main verb is **have**, you usually put *do*, *does* or *did* before the subject. See also p. 177.

Does anyone have a question?
Did you have a good flight?

When **have** means **own** or **possess**, you can put it before the subject, without using *do*, *does* or *did*; but this is less common and a bit formal.

Has he any idea what it's like?

Yes/no questions also have a negative form. **Negative yes/no questions** are almost always contracted. The negative in its contracted form *n't* comes immediately before the subject.

Doesn't he like talking about his childhood?
Can't Peter have one too?
Don't you speak French?
Wouldn't you like to know a little more about this?

If the full negative form *not* is used, it comes immediately after the subject. The full form is very formal.

Does he *not* like talking about his childhood?
Do you *not* want to know what it was about?
Can Peter *not* have one too?

WH- questions

When you want to get a detailed answer, not just *yes* or *no*, you must use a **WH- question** (also called a **nonpolar question**), which allows for many possible answers. The words *who*, *whom*, *whose*, *what*, *which*, *when*, *where*, *why*, and *how* are used to form this sort of question. These words are referred to as **WH-** words. See pp. 92–95.

> **Yes/no:**
> *Did you call* the school? – Yes, I did.
> *Was she* all right in the end? – No/I don't know.
> *Have you seen* Ali yet? – Yes, I have.

> **WH-:**
> *Who* was that man? – He's my geography teacher.
> *What* did he say when you told him the news? – He was too
>   surprised to say anything.
> *When* did you see Ali? – Last Wednesday.
> *Where* is Peter going? – To work.
> *When* did they arrive? – Yesterday.
> *Why* have you stopped going jogging? – The doctor told me to.

WH- words

The **WH-** words are also called **interrogatives**. They are used for **WH-** questions. They can be determiners, adverbs, or pronouns.

WH- determiners

When used as determiners, **what**, **which**, or **whose** can be used to ask questions:

– about nouns,

> **What book** are you reading?
> **Which flight** is he catching?
> **Whose jacket** is this?

– or about the pronoun *one*, *ones*, or other cardinal numbers used as pronouns.

> **Which one** would you like?
> **Which ones** did Ruth want?
> **Which three** are left?

• The determiner **which** can be used in questions about selecting. It can also be used together with the preposition *of if extra* for the same purpose.

> **Which color** shall we use?
> **Which book** sells the most copies?
> **Which of these colors** shall we use?
> *Of all your novels,* **which of them** did you enjoy writing the most?

• The determiner **whose** asks about possession with reference to a person as the possessor.

> **Whose** mother did you say she was?
> **Whose** bag is this?

WH- adverbs

The adverb **WH-** words, **when**, **where**, **how**, and **why**, always make the sentence follow the interrogative word order.

– **When** asks about time.

>   **When** *will they arrive?*
>   **When** *shall I see you again?*

– **Where** asks about place.

>   **Where** *are you going?*
>   **Where** *have you been?*
>   **Where** *is your coat?*

– **How** asks about manner.

>   **How** *did you get here? – We came by train.*
>   **How** *does this thing work?*

– **Why** asks about reasons and purpose. Questions with **why** are usually answered with a clause containing *because* to express reason, or with the *to* infinitive to express purpose.

>   **Why** *is the baby crying? –* **Because** *she's hungry.*
>   **Why** *are you saving your money? –* **To buy** *a bike.*

– **How much** is used for asking about a quantity; **how many** is used for asking about an amount or a countable number of things. Sometimes you can leave out the noun when both speaker and listener know what is being referred to.

>   **How much** *money did they take? – All of it.*
>   **How much** *does it cost? – $4.20.*
>   **How many** *packs do you want? – Twelve, please.*
>   **How many** *do you want? – Twelve, please.*

- **How** can also be used with adjectives such as *old, big, far*, or with adverbs such as *often, soon, quickly* to ask about degree, rate, or timing.

> **How far** *is it to the campground? – About five miles.*
> **How often** *does he come? – Not very often.*

WH- pronouns

The **pronouns** *who*, *whose*, *which*, and *what* can be the subject or object of a verb.

> **Who** *can help me?*
> **Whose** *is the new sports car outside?*
> **Which** *was your best subject in school?*
> **What** *happened next?*
> **What** *have you got to take with you to camp?*

- The interrogative pronoun **whose** is used to ask a question about a person as the possessor of something.

> **Whose** *is the motorbike parked outside?*
> **Whose** *is this?*

- The form **whom** is used as the object of a verb or of a preposition in formal or old-fashioned English.

> **Whom** *did you talk to?*
> **Whom** *would you rather have as a boss?*

Modern English prefers **who** instead of **whom** in all contexts except the most formal ones.

> **Who** *did you talk to?*
> **Who** *would you rather have as a boss?*

When **whom** is used as the object of a preposition, it normally follows the preposition.

> **To whom** *did you speak?*
> **With whom** *did she go?*

When **who** is used, the preposition is placed at the end of the clause.

> **Who** *did you speak* **to?**
> **Who** *did she go* **with?**

The **WH-** subject pronouns are found in the same sentence order as statements:

> **WH- subject pronoun + the main verb**.
> **Who can help** *me?*
> **Whose is** *that motorbike parked outside?*
> **Which was** *your best subject in school?*
> **What happened** *next?*

The **WH-** object pronouns make the sentence take the word order of a question:

> **WH- object pronoun + primary or modal auxiliary + subject + base form** of the verb.
> **What do you have** *to take with you to camp?*
> **What has Jonathan done** *now?*

- The exception to this is in informal spoken English, when the speaker wants to show shock or disbelief.

> *You did* **what?**

Indirect questions

You use indirect questions to ask for information or help. In indirect questions, the subject of the question comes before the verb.

When you ask someone for information, you can use an indirect question beginning with a phrase such as **Could you tell me…** or **Do you know….**

> **Could you tell me** how far it is to the nearest bank?
> **Do you know** where Jarod is?

When you want to ask someone politely to do something, you can use an indirect question after **I wonder**.

> **I wonder** if you can help me.
> **I was wondering** whether you could give me some information.

You also use **I wonder** followed by an indirect question to show what you are thinking about.

> **I wonder** what she'll look like.
> **I wonder** which hotel it was.
> I just **wonder** what you make of all that.

In indirect questions, the subject of the question comes before the verb, just as it does in affirmative statements.

> Do you know where **Ning is**?
> I wonder if **you can help me**.
> She asked me why **I was late**.

You do not normally use the auxiliary **do** in indirect questions.

> Can you remember when **they open** on Sundays?
> I wonder how **he feels** about it.

The auxiliary *do* can be used in indirect questions, but only for emphasis, or to make a contrast with something that has already been said. It is not put before the subject as in yes/no questions.

> *I was beginning to wonder if he **does** do anything.*
> *He wondered whether it really **did** make any difference.*

You use *if* or ***whether*** to introduce indirect questions.

> *I wonder **if** you'd give the children a bath tonight?*
> *I'm writing to ask **whether** you would care to come and visit us.*

Whether is used especially when there is a choice of possibilities.

> *I wonder **whether** it's the police or just a neighbor.*
> *I wonder **whether** that's good for him or not.*

Note that you can put ***or not*** immediately after ***whether***, but not immediately after ***if***.

> *I wonder **whether or not** we are so different from our mothers.*
> *I wonder **if** she'd believe me?*

Sentence tags

Sentence tags (sometimes called **question tags**) are short additions that look like questions, used at the end of a statement. They are used to check that the listener agrees with what the speaker has said, or to signal to the listener that agreement is expected. Sentence tags are very commonly used in spoken English, but not in formal written English.

You can use negative statements with positive question tags, or positive statements with negative question tags. You can also use some question tags to make imperatives more polite.

The tag is added to the end of a statement. If the auxiliary verb **be** or **have** or a **modal** verb is part of the verb phrase in the sentence, then it is used as the verb in the question tag.

> It **isn't** raining again, **is it**?
> You**'ve seen** the program, **haven't you**?
> Well, we **can't jump** over it, **can we**?
> You **will come**, **won't you**?

If the main verb is in the present simple or past simple tense, the tag is made using **do**.

> He doesn't **say** much, **does he**?
> She didn't **call**, **did she**?

In negative tags, **n't** is added to the auxiliary. Note that this contracted form is always used.

> He certainly **likes** eating, **doesn't he**?
> I **slipped up** there, **didn't I**?
> They **went** with you, **didn't they**?

- The formal forms such as, *does he not, did I not, have you not,* sound old-fashioned. They are more common in some regional varieties of English.

The pronoun in the sentence tag must match the subject of the main verb.

> **You** *aren't listening, are* **you**?
> **He** *reads a lot, doesn't* **he**?

Question tags can be **negative**

> *They* **went** *with you,* **didn't they**?

or **positive**.

> *Your father* **doesn't belong to** *the country club,* **does he**?

Normally, when the first part of the sentence is positive, the tag verb will be negative, and vice versa. Sentences in which both parts are positive are less common. These sentences must be used carefully because, with certain tones of voice, they can sound aggressive or judgmental.

> *You* **think** *I'm a fool,* **do** *you*?
> *So you* **smoke** *now,* **do** *you*?

- The same sentence tag may have different meanings depending on the tone of voice that is used with it.

> Falling tone: statement
> *She's gone out, hasn't she?*
>
> Rising tone: question
> *She's gone out, hasn't she?*

The sentence can be a statement of fact or a question, depending on whether your voice rises or falls at the end. However, a question mark is always required.

Question tags are used in the following combinations:

- To say something that the speaker expects the listener will agree with. This doesn't always sound like a question:

  positive main verb + negative tag
  *Melinda **will pass** her driving test this time, **won't she**?*
  *Richard **seems** to have lost interest in everything, **doesn't he**?*

or

  negative main verb + positive tag
  *Jessica **didn't care**, **did she**?*
  *Kerry **hadn't done** enough preparation, **had she**?*

- To point out or remark on something, often something that the listener cannot deny. This frequently sounds more like a question:

  positive main verb + negative tag
  *You've just **bought** a new car, **haven't you**?*
  *Henry **has been** away already this year, **hasn't he**?*

or

  negative main verb + positive tag
  *Dex **hasn't been** to see you, **has he**?*
  *Paula **wasn't** in your class in school, **was she**?*

- To show interest in something. This often repeats part of what the previous speaker has said:

positive main verb + positive tag

*You **saw** him in town, **did you**?*

*So, you **come** from New Jersey, **do you**?*

*So you've just **come back** from skiing, **have you**?*

When a tag is used to show interest in something, the sentence is often begun with *So*. This type of tag can also be used in a challenging manner.

*Oh, so you've **been here** all the time, **have you**?*

After a command, a tag made with *can*, *could*, *shall*, or *would* makes an order more polite.

*Make me a cup of tea, **could you**?*

*Just wait a minute, **would you**?*

*Let's go to the movies, **shall we**?*

The imperative

Commands and orders

The **imperative** is used to give commands and orders. The form of the verb used for the imperative is the **base form** of the main verb, which is used without a subject.

> ***Walk*** *to the corner,* ***turn*** *right, and* ***cross*** *the road.*
> ***Open*** *your mouth and* ***say*** *"Aaaah."*

- Although the main feature of sentences in the imperative is that they have no **grammatical** subject, they do have an **understood** subject, *you*.

The basic form of the imperative remains the same whether it is addressed to one or more people.

> *Come on,* ***Mary****; I'm waiting.*
> *Come on,* ***girls****; you're late.*

There is also a special type of imperative, using ***let's****, that is used when you need to include the speaker. See pp. 104–105.

The word order of a sentence in the imperative is:

> **verb** + **object** (if needed).

The negative imperative is made with ***do*** + ***not*** or ***don't***.

> ***Don't lose*** *that key.*
> ***Do not come back*** *without it!*

The uses of the imperative are as follows.

– To give an order.

> **Go** *away.*
> **Stop** *that.*
> **Keep** *quiet.*

– To give instructions.

> **Don't use** *this spray near an open flame.*
> **Apply** *the glue thinly and* **leave** *it for ten minutes.*

– To give advice or warnings.

> **Don't forget** *to take your passport with you.*
> **Be** *careful!*
> **Don't go** *on the ice.*

– To make an offer or an invitation.

> **Have** *a piece of cake.*
> **Come** *over and* **see** *me some time.*

The imperative of **do** + a **main verb** can be used:

– For polite emphasis.

> **Do take** *your coat off.*

– To be persuasive.

> **Do try** *to eat a little of this; it will be good for you.*

- Note that the imperative is not the only way to form a command or an order. You can also issue a command when you use a sentence in the affirmative or the interrogative.

    I'm certainly not going to get it – ***you get it****.*
    Would you get it*, then? I'm busy.*

Making suggestions

Let's *(**let** + **us**)* + **main verb** is used in the 1st person plural only, especially when you are trying to encourage someone to do something with you.

It includes both the speaker and the hearer, so the subject that is understood is represented by the plural *we*.

    Let's visit *Malcolm this weekend.*
    Please let's go *to the carnival tonight.*
    Let's pool *our resources.*

- Suggestions that start with ***let's*** often end with the sentence tag ***shall we***?

    Let's phone *her now,* ***shall we***?
    Let's go *for a walk after supper,* ***shall we***?

In ordinary English the negative is ***let's not*** + **main verb** or sometimes ***don't let's*** + **main verb**.

    Let's not worry *about that now.*
    Don't let's worry *about that now.*

In formal English, the negative is ***let us not*** + **main verb**.

    Let us not lose *sight of our aims.*

- The uncontracted form **let us** + **main verb** is occasionally used in formal and written English.

    Let us be clear about this.
    Let us hope that this will never happen again.

- The answer to a suggestion with **let's** is normally either yes, let's or no, let's not or sometimes no, don't let's (…).

    Let's phone her now, shall we? – **Yes, let's**.
    Let's phone her now, shall we? – **No, let's not**.
    Let's invite Mokhtar over this weekend. – No, **don't let's** do that.

- You use **let me** followed by the base form of a verb when you are offering to do something for someone.

    Let me take your coat.
    Let me give you a few details.

The subjunctive

The **subjunctive** is used in American English for situations that are improbable or that express a wish. It is also found in certain set phrases and in very formal forms of speech and writing that are common in all dialects.

> God **bless** America
> God **save** the Queen!
> God **help** us!
> Heaven **help** us!
> Heaven **forbid** that that should happen to me.
> **Suffice** it to say he escaped with only a warning.

The present subjunctive

The form in the present tense is exactly the same as the base form in all persons of the verb. That is, there is no **-s** on the 3rd person singular.

The subjunctive can be used in subordinate clauses that follow verbs expressing a desire, a demand, a formal recommendation, or a decision that someone should do something.

> I only ask that he **cease** behaving in this extraordinary manner.
> It is vital that they **be** stopped at once.
> Is it really necessary that she **work** all hours of the day?
> I demand that he **do** something to make up for this.

The clause containing the subjunctive is linked to the main clause with *that*.

The past subjunctive

In written English and in very formal speech, the past subjunctive form **were** is sometimes used with the 1st and 3rd person singular, in place of the normal past form **was**.

The past subjunctive may be used:

– after *if* or *I wish*, to express regret or longing

> *If your father **were** alive he would help you.*
> *If I **were** rich I would buy a Ferrari.*
> *I wish I **were** taller.*
> *If only he **were** here now!*

– or after *as if/as though* and similar expressions, to express doubt or improbability.

> *You talk to him as if he **were** your slave!*
> *Some people behave as though dogs **were** human.*

Many people prefer to use the normal form of the past in this type of sentence. This is acceptable in ordinary English.

> *If your father **was** alive he would help you.*
> *I wish I **was** tall.*
> *If only he **was** here now!*
> *You talk to him as if he **was** your slave!*

Verbs and conditional clauses

Conditional sentences consist of a main clause and a **conditional clause** (sometimes called an *if-clause*). The conditional clause usually begins with *if* or *unless*. The conditional clause can come before or after the main clause.

> We'll be late **if we don't leave now**.
> We'll be late **unless we leave now**.
> **If we don't leave now**, we'll be late.
> **Unless we leave now**, we'll be late.

There are three main types of conditional sentence.

Type 1

The main clause uses *will*, *can*, *may*, or *might* + the **base form** of a main verb. The *if-clause* uses the present simple tense.

> **If you take the first bus**, you'll get there on time.
> She'll be cold **if she doesn't wear a coat**.
> **If you need more helpers**, I can try and get some time off work.

Type 1 sentences refer to the future. They suggest that the action in the main clause is quite likely to happen.

> They **will** not finish their homework unless they start now.
> If you book early, you **will** get a seat.

The use of the modal verb *may* or *might* in the main clause suggests that there is some doubt whether the main verb action will be achieved. See also pp. 194–196.

> If you book early, you **may** get a seat.
> Melanie **might** deliver your message, if you ask her.

Type 2

The main clause uses **would**, **could**, or **might** + the **base form** of a main verb. The **if-clause** uses the past simple tense

> *If Jim **lent** us his car, we could go to the party.*
> *We would save five bucks a day if we **didn't eat** any lunch.*
> *If burglars **broke** into my house, they wouldn't find any money.*
> *Would you be very angry if I **failed** my exam?*

or the past subjunctive.

> *If I **were you**, I'd phone her right away.*

Type 2 sentences refer to an imaginary situation. They suggest that the action in the **if-clause** will probably not happen.

> *If I won the lottery, I would buy a house in Florida.*
>   *(...but I don't think I'll win the lottery.)*
> *If you didn't spend all your money on lottery tickets, you could*
>   *afford a vacation.*
>   *(...but you do spend all your money on lottery tickets.)*

The past subjunctive is often used when you are giving advice to someone, especially about what the person should do.

> *If I **were you**, I'd tell them the truth.*

Type 3

The main clause uses **would**, **could**, or **might** + **have** + the **past participle** of a main verb. The **if-clause** uses the past perfect.

> We could have had a longer vacation, if we **hadn't spent** so much
>   money on the house.
> If I **had known** about the exam, I would have paid more
>   attention in class.

In Type 3 sentences the speaker is looking back from the present to a past time and event. The speaker is talking about what might have happened but did not, either because the wrong thing was done or because nothing was done. People use this type of sentence when they are making excuses, showing regret, blaming, or giving an explanation for the way things are now.

Conditional clauses can also be used to talk about consequences, or to give an opinion about a situation in the following ways.

– The **if-clause** uses the present simple tense and the main clause uses the present simple tense. This is used to refer to universal truths.

> If you **heat** water to 100°C, it **boils**.
> Plants **die** if they **don't get** enough water.

– The **if-clause** uses the present simple tense, and the main clause is in the imperative. This is used to give advice or orders for particular situations or sets of circumstances.

> If the alarm **goes off**, **make** your way outside to the parking lot.
> If a red light **shows** here, **switch off** the machine.

– The **if-clause** uses the present continuous or present simple tense and the main clause uses a modal verb. This is used to make suggestions and give advice.

> If you**'re thinking of** buying a computer, you **could** try mine first.
> You **should** turn down his radio if you **don't want** the neighbors to complain.

– The **if-clause** uses **will/would** and the main clause uses a modal verb.

This is used to make a request or to give a polite order.

> If **you'll** wait a minute, the doctor **can** see you.
> If you **would** sign here, please, I'll be able to send you the books.

Note that a **'d** in the main clause is the contracted form of **would**. However, a **'d** in an **if-clause** is the contracted form of **had**.

I'd have gone if **he'd** invited me.
I **would** have gone **if he had invited me**.
I **would've** gone if **he'd** invited me.

In the main clause, the contracted forms of the modals used in speech and informal writing are:

I'd have	or	I would've
I could've		I might've

Verbs and reporting speech

There are two ways of writing down or reporting what someone said on any occasion. We can repeat the actual words used (**direct speech**),

> Monica said, **"There's nothing we can do about it."**

or we can build the words into our own sentences (**reported speech**).

> Monica said that there was nothing we could do about it.

The words that are reported are normally accompanied by a **reporting verb**.

> Monica **said/declared** that there was nothing we could
>   do about it.
> "There is nothing we can do about it," Monica **replied**.

Another name for reported speech is **indirect speech**.

Direct speech

Direct speech gives the actual words that the speaker used.
It is common in novels and other writing where the actual words
of a speaker are quoted.

> Monica said, **"There's nothing we can do about it."**

The **reporting verb** may come before the words that were actually
spoken, or after them, or at a natural pause inside the reported
sentence.

> ***Monica said***, *"There is nothing we can do about it."*
> *"There is nothing we can do about it,"* ***Monica said***.
> *"It's no good,"* ***Monica said***, *"we'll just have to ask for help."*

- Typical reporting verbs are: *agree*, *answer*, *ask*, *explain*, *inquire*, *say*, *tell*, and *wonder*.

The subject and the reporting verb are sometimes reversed.

> *"There is nothing we can do about it,"* ***said Monica***.

Reported speech

Reported speech or **indirect speech** reports something that was said, but it does not repeat the actual words that the speaker used.

> *Lynn asked whether Pryce had been to the new shopping mall.*
> *Pryce replied that she hadn't, but **she had heard** that there*
>   *were some really cool shops there.*

Reported speech always has two clauses. The words that are spoken are put in a **reported clause**. There is also a **main clause** that contains a **reporting verb**. The main clause with the reporting verb usually comes before the **reported clause**.

> ***Katie told me** that Alix is going to resign.*
> ***Peter asked** whether Mandy was feeling better.*

The reporting verb in the main clause tells us how the sentence was spoken, e.g., *comment, remark, say, tell*. If the reported clause is a **statement**, the main clause is linked to the reported clause by *that*.

> *Mary said **that** her favorite actor was Ben Affleck.*
> *John replied **that** he preferred Scarlett Johansson.*

If the reported clause asks a question, the main verb is a question verb e.g., *ask, inquire, wonder, query*. The link between the main clause and the reported clause is *if* or **whether**.

> *Miriam asked **if** she could borrow Leonie's MP3 player.*
> *Evelyn wondered **whether** the concert would be sold out.*

• The linking word *that* can be left out after most reporting verbs,

> *Jamie told Dad (**that**) he had passed his driving test.*
> *Lance said that Alan had been accepted at drama school.*

but the links *if* or **whether** cannot be left out.

An alternative position for main clauses that would normally have a linking **that**, is after the reported clause. In this case, the link is left out.

> *Harry Potter was on that night,* **Mary said**.

The tense in reported clauses

The verb may also change, e.g. *must* becomes *had to* in reported speech. The most common change is a change of tense. See also Section 2, p. 184.

> "Hello Jake? It's me, Peggy. I've arrived here on time, and I'm going to take a bus to your place. There's one coming now, so I'd better run."

> Peggy rang to say that she'd arrived there on time and **was going to** take a bus to our place. Then she said that one **was** coming at that very moment, so **she had to** run.

A reporting verb in the present tense can be used in the main clause when you report on a letter or on a recent conversation, e.g., a telephone conversation.

> "Hello, Jake? I've arrived here on time, and I'm going to take a bus to your place."
> Peggy has just phoned. She **says** that she has arrived on time and that **she's coming** here by bus.

However, it is more common to use a past tense when reporting speech.

The changes of tense may be summarized as follows:

direct speech	reported speech
present simple	past simple
present continuous	past continuous
present perfect	past perfect
present perfect continuous	past perfect continuous
past simple	past perfect or past simple
future	conditional

Questions

Verb tenses in reported questions undergo the same changes as in statements.

> "Are you ready?"
> He asked (us) if/whether we **were** ready.

> "What time is it?"
> He asked what time it **was**.
> "Where has Jim gone?"
> He wanted to know where Jim **had gone**.

> Reporting verbs for questions include *ask, inquire, want to know,* and *wonder.*

Direct **yes/no** questions are linked to the reporting clause by *if* or **whether**. WH- question words, e.g., *who, when, where,* are used in both direct and indirect questions.

"*Are you tired?*"
He asked (us) if/whether we **were** *tired.*
"*What day is it?*"
He asked what day it **was**.
"*Where has Mom been?*"
He wanted to know where Mom **had been**.

- The word order in a reported question is the same as that of a direct statement. Question order is not used in reported speech, i.e:, no part of the verb comes before the subject.

Orders and requests

Orders are reported with **tell** + **object** + **to infinitive**.

"*Stop calling me names!*"
She **told him to stop** *calling her names.*

Requests for action are reported with **ask** + **object** + **to infinitive**.

"*Please don't leave your things on the floor.*"
She asked us **not to leave** *our things on the floor.*

Requests for objects are reported with **ask for** + **object**.

"*Can I have the salt, please?*"
He **asked for the salt**.

- The reporting verb can be used in the passive.

"*Don't park here, please; it's reserved for the doctors.*"
I was **told not to park** *there.*

Suggestions, advice, and promises

Many verbs can be used for reporting suggestions and similar types of speech. Some of these are:

- *insist on, suggest,* + **present participle**

    > "*Let's go to the zoo.*"
    > **He suggested going to the zoo.**

- *advise, invite, warn* + **direct object** + *not* + **to infinitive**

    > "*I wouldn't buy that one, if I were you.*"
    > She advised me **not to buy** that one.

- *refuse, threaten* + **to infinitive**

    > "*I'm not telling you!*"
    > She **refused to tell** me.

- *offer, promise* + **to infinitive**

    > "*Don't worry; I'll help you.*"
    > He **promised to help** me.

A–Z of important verbs

account [ə'kaunt]

accounts	3rd person present
accounting	present participle
accounted	past tense & past participle

PHRASAL VERB

account for something

to explain something or give the reason for it □ *How do you account for the differences in the two figures?*

act [ækt]

acts	3rd person present
acting	present participle
acted	past tense & past participle

INTRANSITIVE

1 to do something for a particular purpose □ *The police acted to stop the fight.*
2 to behave in a particular way □ *The youths were acting suspiciously.* □ *He acts as if I'm not there.*
3 to have a part in a play or a film □ *He acted in many films, including 'Titanic'.*

PHRASAL VERBS

act out

to behave badly because of emotional problems □ *Kids act out for a reason, the boy could be jealous of his sister.*

act up

to misbehave or not work properly □ *The engine thruster has been acting up for eight months.*

add [æd]

adds	3rd person present
adding	present participle
added	past tense & past participle

TRANSITIVE

1 to put one thing with another thing □ *Add the cheese to the sauce.*
2 to say something more □ *"He's very angry," Mr. Smith added.*

PHRASAL VERBS

add something up

to find the total of various numbers or amounts □ *Add up the number of hours you spent on the task.*

add up to something

to form a total □ *Altogether, the three bills add up to $2,456.*

answer ['ænsər]

answers	3rd person present
answering	present participle
answered	past tense & past participle

1 TRANSITIVE AND INTRANSITIVE to say something back to someone who has spoken to you
Ⓣ *I asked him but he didn't answer.*
Ⓘ *Williams answered that he didn't know.*
2 TRANSITIVE AND INTRANSITIVE to pick up the telephone when it rings
Ⓘ *Why didn't you answer when I phoned?*
Ⓣ *She didn't answer the telephone.*
3 TRANSITIVE AND INTRANSITIVE to open the door when you hear a knock or the bell
Ⓘ *I knocked and Mary answered the door.*
4 TRANSITIVE to write or say what you think is the correct answer to a question in a test □ *Before you start to answer the questions, read the whole test carefully.*

PHRASAL VERBS

answer for someone or something

to be responsible for someone or for something that has happened □ *This guy gets away with everything but never is forced to answer for it when found out.*

answer to someone

to explain your actions to someone □ *The press is demanding that the mayor answer to the voters for this controversial appointment.*

arise ✪ [ə'raiz]

arises	3rd person present
arising	present participle
arose	past tense
arisen	past participle

INTRANSITIVE to begin to exist □ *When the opportunity finally arose, thousands of workers left.* □ *I called him at home because a problem had arisen at work.*

awake ✪ [ə'weik]

awakes	3rd person present
awaking	present participle
awoke	past tense
awoken	past participle

TRANSITIVE AND INTRANSITIVE to stop sleeping or to make someone stop sleeping (*literary*)

☐ *I was awoken by the sound of many voices.*

☐ *At midnight he awoke and listened to the radio for awhile.*

back [bæk]

backs	3rd person present
backing	present participle
backed	past tense & past participle

TRANSITIVE AND INTRANSITIVE

1 to move backwards or to move a vehicle backwards

☐ *He backed his car out of the driveway.*

☐ *The car backed out of the garage.*

2 to support someone ☐ *We told them what we wanted to do, and they agreed to back us.*

PHRASAL VERBS

back away

to move away from someone or something, often because you are frightened ☐ *James stood up, but the girl backed away.*

back down

to withdraw a claim, assertion, or intention that is opposed ☐ *Australia on Friday backed down on a hefty 40 percent tax on mining.*

back off

to move away from someone or something, in order to avoid problems

☐ *When she saw me she backed off, looking worried.*

back out or back out of something

to decide not to do something that you had agreed to do ☐ *They've backed out of the project.* ☐ *He asked her to marry him, but she backed out.*

back something up

1 to show that something is true ☐ *He didn't have any proof to back up his story.*

2 to make a copy of a computer file so that you can use it if the original file is lost ☐ *Make sure you back up your files every day.*

bank [bæŋk]

banks	3rd person present
banking	present participle
banked	past tense & past participle

PHRASAL VERB

bank on someone or something

to rely on someone or something

☐ *Everyone is banking on his recovery.*

be

➡ See Key Verb entry on p. 122

be able to

➡ See Key Verb entry on p. 127

bear ✪ [bɛəʳ]

bears	3rd person present
bearing	present participle
bore	past tense
borne	past participle

TRANSITIVE

1 to accept an unpleasant experience

☐ *She bore her illness bravely.*

2 to be able to support the weight of someone or something ☐ *The ice was not thick enough to bear their weight.*

3 to bear the cost of something means to pay for it ☐ *The cost will be borne by the government.*

4 can't bear someone or something

to dislike someone or something very much ☐ *She can't bear to see the cats — or any other animal — go hungry* ☐ *I can't bear her for more than a few minutes.*

PHRASAL VERB

bear with someone

to wait patiently for someone to finish doing something ☐ *Bear with me, Frank, just let me explain.*

be [bi]

IRREGULAR AUXILIARY AND LINKING VERB

am	1st person singular present
are	2nd person singular and plural present,
	1st person plural present,
	3rd person plural present
is	3rd person singular present
was	1st and 3rd person singular past
were	2nd person singular past and plural past
being	present participle
been	past participle

Be is an auxiliary verb and a main verb. As an auxiliary verb, **be** is used to form the continuous and the passive. As a main verb, **be** is a linking verb that joins a subject to its complement.

*I **am** late.*	*We **are** late.*
*You **are** late.*	*You **are** late.*
*He **is** late.*	*They **are** late.*

*I **was** late.*	*We **were** late.*
*You **were** late.*	*You **were** late.*
*She **was** late.*	*They **were** late.*

*He is **being** very helpful these days.*
*We have **been** ready for an hour.*

Contracted forms

In spoken English, the present simple tense forms of **be** are often contracted. Note that the contracted form of *they are* is spelled *they're* (not *their*, which is the possessive form of **they**).

I'm here.   **We're** here.
You're here.   **You're** here.
He's here.   **They're** here.

Making negatives

You make a negative with **be** by adding *not* immediately after it. In spoken English, some forms of **be** also have contracted negative forms. Some of these forms make the negative stronger.

Emphasizes the negative

*I'm **not*** late.
*You **aren't*** late.   *You'**re not*** late.
*He **isn't*** late.   *He'**s not*** late.
*We **aren't*** late.   *We'**re not*** late.
*They **aren't*** late.   *They'**re not*** late.

*I **wasn't*** late.
*You **weren't*** late.
*He **wasn't*** late.
*We **weren't*** late.
*They **weren't*** late.

Auxiliary verb uses of *be*

The main uses of **be** as an auxiliary verb are to form the past and present continuous and the passive.

1 **Be** is used with another verb to form the past or present continuous. Continuous forms of main verbs use the appropriate form of **be**, present or past, followed by the **-ing** form of the main verb.

> *This is happening everywhere in the country.*
> *She was driving to work when the accident happened.*

2 **Be** is used with another verb to form the passive. The passive form of a main verb uses the appropriate form of **be** followed by the past participle of the main verb.

> *He is expected to retire soon.*
> *Her husband was killed in a car crash.*

3 **Be** is used with an infinitive to show that something is planned to happen. This is a rather formal use, which often appears in news reports.

> *The talks are to begin tomorrow.*
> *The President is to visit Hungary in October.*

Main verb senses of *be*

The verb **be** is also used as a main verb. It is commonly found joining a subject to its complement.

1 **Be** is used for introducing more information or giving an opinion about a subject.

She's my mother.
He is a very kind man.

2 You use **be** with **it** as a subject when you are talking about time, distance, weather, or cost. In this use, **be** is always singular.

It was too cold for swimming.
Hurry up, it's eight thirty!
Is it? I didn't know it was so late.
It's thirty miles to Gafney.
Come and visit us. It's not very far.
It's cold today but it isn't wet.
It's very expensive to live in Boston.

3 **Be** is used in expressions like **there is** and **there are** to say that something exists. **Be** may be singular or plural depending on the number or countability of the noun after it. **Be** is also sometimes contracted.

There's a spare toothbrush in the medicine cabinet.
There was a cold wind blowing.
There isn't enough gas for the trip.
There are several gas stations on the way, aren't there?
There is very little traffic this morning.

4 **Be** is used for talking about feelings and states. For this you use the simple form of the verb with an adjective.

I am delighted with the news, but he is not happy.
She was busy so she was not able to see me.

5 **Be** is used for talking about people's behavior. For this you use the continuous form of the verb with an adjective.

I am not being slow, I am being careful.
You were being very disrespectful to your mom when I came
  downstairs.

To make the continuous form of the main verb **be**, you have to use **be** twice: once as an auxiliary and once as a main verb.

> You **are being** so annoying!
> I know I **am being** silly, but I'm frightened.

You make the question form of clauses with the verb **be** by putting the appropriate form of **be** immediately in front of the subject.

> **Are** you better now?
> **Is** he free this morning?
> **Was** he cooking dinner when you arrived?

be able to ['eɪbəl]

PHRASAL MODAL VERB

You use **be able to** in the present, past, and future tenses. The appropriate forms and tenses of **be** are used with **able to** and the base form of the main verb to talk about ability.

Sometimes *could*, rather than **be able to**, is used to talk about ability in the past. **Be able to** tends to be used more for talking about particular occasions, and *could* tends to be used for general statements about ability in the past, but there is no strict rule:

> When I was younger, I *could* run very fast.
> I *wasn't able to* run to the bus stop before the bus drove off.

> I *wasn't able to* finish my essay last night.
> I *couldn't* finish my essay last night.

> When you were in college, *could you* usually get your work done on time?
> When you were in college, *were you* usually *able to* get your work done on time?

See pp.140–144 for other uses of *could*.

Question forms

You form questions with **be able to** by putting the subject between **be** and **able to**, followed by the base form of the main verb.

> Are you able to give me a ride to the airport tonight?
> Was Mark able to repair the washing machine?

Main senses

1 If someone **is able to** do something, they have skills or qualities that make it possible for them to do it.

> *A ten-year-old should be able to prepare a simple meal.*
> *They were able to work well together.*

2 If someone **is able to** do something, they have enough freedom, power, time, or money to do it.

> *If I get this job, I'll be able to buy a new car.*
> *It would be nice to be able to afford to retire next year.*

beat ❂ [bit]

beats	3rd person present
beating	present participle
beat	past tense
beaten	past participle

1 TRANSITIVE to hit someone or something many times □ *They beat him, and left him on the ground.*

2 INTRANSITIVE to make a regular sound and movement □ *I felt my heart beating faster.*

3 TRANSITIVE to mix food quickly with a spoon or a fork □ *Beat the eggs and sugar together.*

4 TRANSITIVE to defeat someone in a competition or an election □ *The Red Sox beat the Yankees 5–2 last night.*

PHRASAL VERBS

beat someone up

to hit or kick someone many times □ *I was beaten up and lost a lot of blood.*

beat yourself up

to blame yourself for something bad that has happened *(informal)* □ *Tell them you don't want to do it any more. Don't beat yourself up about it.*

become ❂ [bi'kʌm]

becomes	3rd person present
becoming	present participle
became	past tense
become	past participle

LINKING VERB to start to be something or someone □ *The weather became cold and wet in October.* □ *Since I last saw Teresa, she has become a teacher.*

begin ❂ [bi'gɪn]

begins	3rd person present
beginning	present participle
began	past tense
begun	past participle

TRANSITIVE

1 to start doing something □ *Jack stood up and began moving around the room.* □ *David began to look angry.*

2 to start to happen, or to start something

T *The problems began last November.*

T *He has just begun his second year in college.*

be going to
→ See *Key Verb* entry on p. 130

be meant to
→ See *Key Verb* entry on p. 132

bend ❂ [bɛnd]

bends	3rd person present
bending	present participle
bent	past tense & past participle

1 INTRANSITIVE to move the top part of your body down and forward □ *I bent and kissed her cheek.*

2 TRANSITIVE AND INTRANSITIVE to change the position of something so that it is no longer straight, or to be changed in this way

T *Remember to bend your legs when you do this exercise.*

I *She looked at the trees, their branches bending to meet the grass.*

3 INTRANSITIVE to change direction to form a curve □ *The road bends slightly to the right.*

be supposed to
→ See *Key Verb* entry on p. 134

bet ❂ [bɛt]

bets	3rd person present
betting	present participle
bet	past tense & past participle

TRANSITIVE AND INTRANSITIVE

1 to give someone money and say what you think the result of a race or a sports game will be. If you are correct, they give you your money back with some extra money, but if you are wrong they keep your money.

I *My mother does not let me bet on horse races.*

T *I bet $20 on a horse called Bright Boy.*

2 I bet used for showing that you are sure something is true *(informal)* □ *I bet you were good at sports when you were in school.*

be going to [goʊɪŋ]

PHRASAL MODAL VERB

You use **be going to** for talking about intentions, and for making predictions. You use the appropriate form of **be** with **going to** and the base form of a main verb.

> *I am going to/I'm going to join the Peace Corps when I finish college.*

Negative forms

> *I am not going to/I'm not going to marry Peter. We've canceled the wedding.*

> *I was not going to/I wasn't going to tell you; I didn't want to upset you.*

Question forms

> *Are you going to come to the movie with us?*
> *Aren't you going to come to the movie with us?*

> *Were you going to tell us the truth?*
> *Weren't you going to tell us the truth?*

Main senses

1 **Be going to** is used for talking about something that will happen in the future, usually quite soon.

> *You're going to enjoy this!*
> *Your party is going to be a great success.*
> *Are they going to be all right?*

2 **Be going to** is used for saying that someone intends to do something, or is determined to do something. You can also talk about past intentions by using the past form of **be**.

> *I'm going to go to bed.*
> *Robert says that he's going to be a doctor when he grows up.*
> *Linda was going to come to the concert, but she had to work instead.*

Compare the use of **be going to** and *will*. You use **be going to** when you are expressing your intention to do something in the future. You use *will* to express a decision that you make at the time you are speaking.

> *"I'm going to have coffee. Would you like some?"—*
> *"Yes, thanks, I'll have some."*

See also p.217 for this use of *will*.

3 **Be going to** is used for talking about things that have already been decided.

> *"Is Caroline going to move to Atlanta?"—"Yes, she is."*
> *"Are they coming by bus?"—"No, they said they were going to take a taxi."*

4 **Be going to** is used for making a prediction about the future (often the very near future), based on something in the present. You can also talk about past predictions by using the past form of **be**.

> *If you don't hurry up, we're going to be late.*
> *He was obviously going to fail his driving test.*

be meant to [mɛnt]

PHRASAL MODAL VERB

You use **be meant to** for talking about things that you expect to happen, or that ought to happen. It is also used to talk about the reputation of a particular person or thing. You use the appropriate form of **be** with **meant to** and the base form of a main verb.

> *He is meant to arrive this evening.*
> *This is meant to be the best hotel in Fargo.*

Negative forms

> *I am/I'm not meant to be here. I should be at school.*
> *Reba wasn't meant to know about this.*

Question forms

> *Are you meant to be doing that?*
> *Was he meant to arrive at six?*

Main senses

1 You use **be meant to** for talking about things that you expect to happen, or that ought to happen.

> *Parties are meant to be fun.*
> *The process is meant to be voluntary, easy, and all-inclusive.*

2 **Be meant to** is used for talking about the intention or purpose of something.

> *The ad is meant to suggest that the car is fuel-efficient.*
> *The expanded parking apron is meant to serve private planes flying to the island.*

bind ✪ [baind]

binds	3rd person present
binding	present participle
bound	past tense & past participle

TRANSITIVE to tie rope or string around something to hold it firmly □ *Bind the ends of the rope with thread.* □ *They bound his hands behind his back.*

bite ✪ [bait]

bites	3rd person present
biting	present participle
bit	past tense
bitten	past participle

TRANSITIVE AND INTRANSITIVE

1 to use your teeth to cut into or through something

Ⓣ *William bit the cookie in two.*

Ⓘ *I watched her bite into an apple.*

2 If a snake or an insect bites, it makes a mark or a hole in your skin with a sharp part of its body.

Ⓘ *Do these flies bite?*

Ⓣ *He was bitten by a snake but made a full recovery.*

3 bite your lip or **bite your tongue** to stop yourself from saying something, because it would be wrong to do so □ *Instead of biting my lip, I had to speak out.* □ *He bit his tongue to prevent himself from swearing aloud.*

black [blæk]

blacks	3rd person present
blacking	present participle
blacked	past tense & past participle

PHRASAL VERB

black out

to become unconscious for a short time □ *For a moment he thought he was going to black out.*

bleed ✪ [blid]

bleeds	3rd person present
bleeding	present participle
bled	past tense & past participle

INTRANSITIVE to lose blood from a part of your body □ *Ian's lip was bleeding.* □ *That night, the man bled to death.*

blow ✪ [blou]

blows	3rd person present
blowing	present participle
blew	past tense
blown	past participle

1 INTRANSITIVE When a wind blows, the air moves. □ *A cold wind was blowing.*

2 INTRANSITIVE to send out air from your mouth □ *Danny blew on his fingers to warm them.*

3 TRANSITIVE to send air from your mouth into an object so that it makes a sound □ *When the referee blows his whistle, the game begins.*

4 blow your nose to force air out of your nose in order to clear it □ *He took out a handkerchief and blew his nose.*

PHRASAL VERBS

blow something out

to blow at a flame so that it stops burning □ *I blew out the candle.*

blow up or blow something up

1 to explode, or to destroy something by an explosion □ *Three cars in the parking lot blew up.* □ *He was jailed for trying to blow up a building.*

2 to fill something with air □ *Can you help me blow up the balloons?*

boot [but]

boots	3rd person present
booting	present participle
booted	past tense & past participle

TRANSITIVE to make a computer ready to start working □ *Put the CD into the drive and boot the machine.*

PHRASAL VERB

boot up or boot something up

If a computer boots up, or if you boot it up, it starts working so that you can use it. □ *Go over to your computer and boot it up.* □ *He left the machine to boot up while he looked around.*

be supposed to [səˈpouzd, səˈpoust]

PHRASAL MODAL VERB

You use **be supposed to** for talking about things that are planned or expected, and situations that people think are true, although they may not be. The appropriate form of the verb **be** is used with **supposed to** and the base form of the main verb.

> *I am supposed to meet Anita at 1:30 pm.*
> *Simon is supposed to be very smart.*

You can use **supposed to** in questions and negatives. Note that when you form a question with **supposed to**, it is in the negative when the person asking the question is expecting the answer "Yes".

> *Aren't you supposed to be at school? (not **Are** you supposed to be at school?)*
> *You weren't supposed to tell John. It was a secret.*

Main senses

1 **Be supposed to** is used for saying that something is planned or expected. Sometimes this use suggests that the thing does not actually happen in the way that was planned or expected. Here you use the appropriate form of the verb **be** and **supposed to**, followed by the base form of the main verb.

> *The children are supposed to be in bed by eight o'clock. Why are they still up?*
> *You are supposed to be in school. What are you doing here?*

2   You use **be supposed to** for saying that you have heard
    something is true.

> I haven't read his latest novel but it's supposed to be
>   really good.
> They are supposed to have gotten married in Mexico last
>   weekend.

3   You use **be supposed to** for showing that you are annoyed by
    someone's attitude or behavior.

> How can you say that? You're supposed to be my friend!
> What am I supposed to have done wrong now?

4   You use **be supposed to** in questions to confirm or find out
    what you or someone else should do in a particular situation.
    In this sense, the meaning is similar to **should**.

> When it says "Accept all changes" am I supposed to click
>   "yes" or "no"?
> Are the students supposed to leave their bookbags in their
>   lockers?

break ✪ [breɪk]

breaks	3rd person present
breaking	present participle
broke	past tense
broken	past participle

1 INTRANSITIVE to separate suddenly into pieces, often after falling or hitting something □ *The plate broke.*

2 TRANSITIVE to make something separate into pieces, often by dropping or hitting it □ *I've broken a bone in my left foot.*

3 TRANSITIVE AND INTRANSITIVE to damage something so that it stops working, or to be damaged and stop working

Ⓣ *I've broken my cell phone so I need a new one.*
Ⓘ *My washing machine has broken.*

4 TRANSITIVE to do something that you should not do because it is against a law, promise or agreement □ *She says you broke a promise to her.*

PHRASAL VERBS

break down

1 to stop working □ *Their car broke down.*
2 to start crying □ *I broke down and cried.*

break in

to get into a building by force □ *The robbers broke in and stole $8,000.*

break out

to begin suddenly □ *He was 29 when war broke out.*

break something off

to remove one part of a thing from the rest of it by breaking it □ *Grace broke off a large piece of bread.*

break up

to separate into pieces or separate parts □ *When the Soviet Union broke up, people went to London, France, Israel, and Spain and started buying real estate.*

break up or break up with someone

to end a relationship □ *My girlfriend has broken up with me.* □ *We broke up last year.*

breathe ✪ [briːð]

breathes	3rd person present
breathing	present participle
breathed	past tense & past participle

INTRANSITIVE to take air into the lungs and let it out again □ *The air was so hot, it was really hard to breathe.*

PHRASAL VERBS

breathe in

to take some air into your lungs □ *Now breathe in through your nose.*

breathe out

to send air out of your lungs through your nose or mouth □ *As you breathe out, lift your arms straight out to the side.*

breed ✪ [briːd]

breeds	3rd person present
breeding	present participle
bred	past tense & past participle

1 TRANSITIVE to keep male and female animals so that they will produce babies □ *His father bred horses in a field behind our house.*

2 INTRANSITIVE When animals breed, they produce babies. □ *Birds usually breed in the spring.*

bring ✪ [brɪŋ]

brings	3rd person present
bringing	present participle
brought	past tense & past participle

> **Bring** or **take**? **Bring** gives the idea of movement toward the speaker and **take** gives the idea of movement away from the speaker.

TRANSITIVE

1 to have someone or something with you when you come to a place
□ *Remember to bring an old shirt to wear when we paint.* □ *Can I bring Susie to the party?*

2 to get something that someone wants and take it to them □ *He poured a glass of milk for Sarah and brought it to her.*

bring someone up
to take care of a child until it is an adult □ *She brought up four children.*

bring something about
to cause something to happen □ *This is the only way to bring about change.*

bring something back
to return something □ *Could you please bring back those books that I lent you?*

bring something in
1 to earn money □ *My job brings in about $36,000 a year.*
2 to introduce a new law or system □ *Qatar is set to bring in a law on safe management of the country's fast accumulating stock of hazardous electronic waste.*

bring something out
to produce something and sell it □ *He's now brought out a book.*

bring something up
to introduce a subject into a discussion or conversation □ *Why are you bringing it up now?*

See note at **grow up**.

build ✪ [bɪld]
builds	3rd person present
building	present participle
built	past tense & past participle

TRANSITIVE to make something by joining different things together □ *They built a hotel there forty years ago.*

bump [bʌmp]
bumps	3rd person present
bumping	present participle
bumped	past tense & past participle

TRANSITIVE to accidentally hit something or someone while you are moving □ *She bumped her head on a low branch.*

bump into someone
to meet someone you know by chance □ *I bumped into Lisa in the supermarket yesterday.*

burn ✪ [bɜrn]
burns	3rd person present
burning	present participle
burned, burnt	past tense & past participle

The past tense and past participle is **burned** in American English, and **burned** or **burnt** in British English.

1 TRANSITIVE to destroy or damage something with fire □ *She burned her old love letters.*

2 TRANSITIVE to injure a part of your body by fire or by something very hot □ *Take care not to burn your fingers.*

3 INTRANSITIVE to produce heat or fire □ *Forty forest fires were burning in Alberta yesterday.*

4 INTRANSITIVE If something is burning, it is being destroyed by fire. □ *When I arrived, one of the cars was still burning.*

5 TRANSITIVE to copy something onto a CD □ *I have the equipment to burn audio CDs.*

burn down or burn something down
to destroy a building by fire, or to be destroyed in this way □ *The old prison had been burned down one night.* □ *Her house burned down with all her personal possessions in it.*

burn out
to stop burning because there is no more fuel □ *Most of the fires are expected to burn out by the weekend.*

burn out or burn someone out
To become exhausted and unable to continue because of overwork, or to cause this in someone □ *Some people burn out after only a few months in this job.* □ *Patrick explained he is currently taking a break, as his accelerated program burned him out.*

burst ✪ [bɜrst]

bursts	3rd person present
bursting	present participle
burst	past tense & past participle

TRANSITIVE AND INTRANSITIVE

1 to suddenly break open and release air or another substance

Ⓘ *The driver lost control of his car when a tire burst.*

Ⓣ *The river burst its banks in several places.*

2 burst into flames to suddenly start burning strongly □ *The plane burst into flames when it crashed.*

3 burst into tears to suddenly start crying □ *I started shouting at her and she burst into tears.*

PHRASAL VERB

burst out

to suddenly start laughing, crying, or making another noise □ *The class burst out laughing.*

buy ✪ [bai]

buys	3rd person present
buying	present participle
bought	past tense & past participle

> **Buy** or **pay**? If you **buy** something, you get it by paying money for it. *Gary's bought a new car.* If you **pay** someone, you give someone money for a product or a service. *I paid the taxi driver.*

TRANSITIVE to get something by paying money for it □ *He could not afford to buy a house.* □ *Lizzie bought herself a bike.*

call [kɑl]

calls	3rd person present
calling	present participle
called	past tense & past participle

1 TRANSITIVE to give someone or something a particular name □ *I wanted to call the dog Mufty.*

2 TRANSITIVE to say something in a loud voice □ *Someone called his name.*

3 TRANSITIVE to telephone someone

□ *Would you call me as soon as you find out?*

4 INTRANSITIVE to make a short visit somewhere □ *A salesman called at the house.*

PHRASAL VERBS

call for something

1 to require, in order to progress or succeed □ *The concept ultimately calls for people to transcend the limits of biology by using technology to develop into something more advanced and intelligent.*

2 to suggest strongly that something should happen or be done □ *Greek public sector union ADEDY called for a strike on July 15 to protest labor reforms.*

call someone in

to request that someone come to you

□ *The commanding officer called her in and said look, someone is spreading nasty rumors.*

call on someone

to visit someone for a short time □ *Sofia was intending to call on Miss Kitts.*

call someone back

to telephone someone in return for a call they made to you □ *I'll call you back.*

call something out

to order a military body to be ready for action or an emergency □ *Arne Carlson did what governors do in an emergency – called out the National Guard.*

call someone up

to telephone someone □ *When I'm in Pittsburgh, I'll call him up.*

call something off

to cancel an event that has been planned □ *He called off the trip.*

calm [kɑːm]

calms	3rd person present
calming	present participle
calmed	past tense & past participle

PHRASAL VERBS

calm down

to become less upset or excited □ *Calm down and listen to me.*

calm someone down

to make someone less upset or excited
□ *I'll try to calm him down.*

can

➡ See *Key Verb* entry on p. 140

cancel [ˈkænsəl]

cancels	3rd person present
canceling	present participle
canceled	past tense & past participle

In British and sometimes in American
English, the present participle, past
tense, and past participle are spelled
cancelling, cancelled.

TRANSITIVE AND INTRANSITIVE to stop
something from happening
Ⓣ *Many trains have been canceled today.*
Ⓘ *If you cancel, a fee may be charged.*

PHRASAL VERB

cancel something out

to have an opposite effect to the effect of
something else and so to produce no real
effect □ *One error shouldn't cancel out the
good work they've done.*

care [kɛr]

cares	3rd person present
caring	present participle
cared	past tense & past participle

INTRANSITIVE to be interested in
someone or something, or to think they
are very important □ *I don't care what she
said about me.*

PHRASAL VERB

care for someone

1 to love someone □ *He still cares for you.*
2 to take care of someone □ *A nurse cares
for David in his home.*

carry [ˈkɛri]

carries	3rd person present
carrying	present participle
carried	past tense & past participle

TRANSITIVE

1 to hold something in your hand and
take it with you □ *He was carrying a briefcase.*

2 to always have something with you
□ *You have to carry a passport.*
3 to take someone or something
somewhere □ *Flights carrying food and
medicine left yesterday.*

PHRASAL VERBS

carry on

to continue to do something □ *The
teacher carried on despite her headache.*

carry something out

to do and complete a task □ *They carried
out tests in the laboratory.*

cast ✪ [kæst]

casts	3rd person present
casting	present participle
cast	past tense & past participle

TRANSITIVE

1 to choose an actor for a particular role
□ *He was cast as a college professor.*
2 to throw something somewhere
(literary) □ *He cast the stone away.*
3 If you cast your eyes or cast a look
somewhere, you look there. *(written)*
□ *Adam cast his eyes over his notes again.*

PHRASAL VERBS

cast about

to try to find something □ *I cast about for
a place to live.*

cast around

to try to find something □ *She was casting
around for an excuse not to go to the party.*

cast someone or something
aside

to get rid of someone or something
□ *In America we seem to cast aside our old
people.*

catch ✪ [kætʃ]

catches	3rd person present
catching	present participle
caught	past tense & past participle

TRANSITIVE

1 to find a person or animal and not allow
them to escape □ *Police say they are
confident of catching the man.* □ *Where did
you catch the fish?*

can [kən, STRONG kæn] and
could [kʌd, STRONG kʊd]

MODAL VERBS

You use **can** and **could** to talk about ability.

You use **can** + the base form of a main verb in the present. You can also use a present form of **be** + **able to** + the base form of a main verb. Note that **can** is used for talking about ability in a more general way than **be able to**, which is usually used for talking about someone's ability to do something at a particular time.

> *They can all read and write.*
> *Are you able to walk to the car, or shall I help you?*

You use **could** + the base form of a main verb to talk about the past. You can also use a simple past form of **be** + **able to** + the base form of a main verb. Note the difference in meaning in the examples below. In the first example, **could** is used because we are talking about general ability. In the second example, we use **was able to** because we are talking about ability in a particular situation. This is not a very strict rule, though.

> *She was so good at math that she could solve equations in her head.*
> *After a check-up at the hospital Peter was able to go home.*

To talk about the future, you use **can** + the base form of a main verb. You can also use **will/shall** + **be able to** + the base form of a main verb.

> *Can we go to see a movie tonight?*
> *Will Granddad be able to climb these steep stairs?*

See also pp.127–128 for **be able to**.

We also use **can** and **could** to talk about possibility. Note the difference in use: **could** refers to a particular occasion and **can** refers to more general situations.

> *Many jobs could be lost in this recession.*
> *Too much salt in the diet can be harmful.*

Making negatives

You use **cannot** and **could not** to make negative statements. In spoken English, we usually shorten these to **can't** and **couldn't**. **Cannot** or **could not** come between the subject and the main verb.

> *He **cannot/can't** read or write.*
> *I **could not/couldn't** read or write.*

Main senses

1 You use **can** and **could** for saying that you have or had the ability or opportunity to do something.

> *Morry can speak French fluently.*
> *You can come over for dinner whenever you like.*
> *I could see that something was wrong.*

2 **Can** and **could** are used with words such as **smell**, **see**, **hear** and **taste**.

> *I can smell smoke. Can you?*
> *We could hear a car driving past.*

3 **Can** and **could** are used for making informal requests. Using **could** rather than **can** makes the request more tentative (that is, you want to be more careful, because you are asking for something that the other person may not want to do or give you). Compare these uses with **may**, which is more formal.

> Can I have a look at that book?
> Could I borrow the car tomorrow evening, Mom?
> May I ask you something, Mr. Murrahid?

4 You use **can** and **could** for asking for, or giving, permission to do something, or for saying that you have permission to do something. Compare these uses with *may*, which is more formal.

> Can I go to the party this weekend, Dad?
> Dad said that I could go to the party.
> May I suggest something else?

Note that when you are changing sentences from direct to reported speech, **can** usually becomes **could**.

> "I can do it," said Dan.
> Dan said that he could do it.

5 **Can** and **could** are used for talking about the possibility of an action in the future, especially when the possibility relates to plans or projects. Compare the examples below. In the example with **could**, the action is less likely to take place.

> We can go to Montreal next week since you are free.
> We could go to Montreal next week if you are free.

6 **Can** and **could** are used for talking about the possibility of an action in the present (using **can**) or past (using **could**).

> We can swim here; it's safe.
> She discovered she couldn't have children.
> He can be very charming when he wants to.
> He could be very charming when he wanted to.

7 **Could** is used for talking about actions that were possible but that did not happen. Here, you use *could have* followed by the past participle of the main verb.

Mary could have stopped them fighting but she didn't.
You could have told me the truth!
He could have made a lot of money as a lawyer.
You should be more careful! You could have broken your leg!

8 **Can** and **could** are used in conditional clauses. Note that **can** is used when the situation in the **if** clause is likely to happen, and **could** when the situation in the **if** clause is unlikely or impossible.

If Louisa is coming, she can look after the children for a while.
If I could afford it, I'd buy a new car.

9 You use **cannot** and **can't** for saying that you are certain that something is not true, or that something will not happen.

Things can't be that bad.
You cannot be serious! That's a crazy idea.

10 You use **can** and **could** when you are politely interrupting someone.

Can I interrupt you just for a minute?
Could I just say something?

Can (but not **could**) is also used in the following ways:

1 to make an offer (generally in the form of a question). Compare this use with **may**, which is more formal.

Can I help you?
May I assist you, sir?

2 to say that something is sometimes true, or is true in some circumstances.

Exercising on your own can be boring.
Coral can be yellow, blue, or green.

3 in questions with **how** to indicate that you feel strongly about something.

> *How can you expect me to believe you?*

Could (but not **can**) is also used in the following ways.

1 to make polite offers and suggestions.

> *I could call the doctor.*
> *Couldn't you have a talk with your brother?*

2 to show that something is possibly true, or that it may possibly happen.

> *It could snow again tonight.*
> *"Where's Jack?"—"I'm not sure; he could be in his bedroom."*

3 to ask about or make guesses about actions that have recently taken place. Here, you use **could** + **have** followed by the past participle of the main verb. This use is often found in questions.

> *Who could have broken the window?*
> *He could have seen the lights out and decided that no one was home.*

2 to take and hold an object that is moving through the air □ *I jumped up to catch the ball.*

3 to get part of your body stuck somewhere accidentally □ *I caught my finger in the car door.*

4 to get on a bus, train, or plane in order to travel somewhere □ *We caught the bus on the corner of the street.*

5 to see or find someone doing something wrong □ *They caught him with $30,000 cash in a briefcase.*

6 to become ill with an illness □ *Keep warm, or you'll catch a cold.*

PHRASAL VERBS

catch on or catch on with someone

to become popular □ *Photography began to catch on as a hobby.* □ *The play didn't catch on with a wider audience.*

catch up or catch up with someone

1 to reach someone in front of you by walking faster than them □ *I stopped and waited for her to catch up.* □ *She hurried to catch up with him.*

2 to reach the same level as someone else □ *You'll have to work hard to catch up.* □ *She'll soon catch up with the other students.*

check [tʃɛk]

checks	3rd person present
checking	present participle
checked	past tense & past participle

TRANSITIVE AND INTRANSITIVE

1 to make sure that something is correct
Ⓣ *Check the meanings of the words in a dictionary.*
Ⓘ *I think there is an age limit, but I'll check.*

2 to put a check mark (✓) next to something to show that it has been selected or dealt with □ *Frequently, it is men who check answer (b).*

PHRASAL VERBS

check in

to tell the person at the desk of an airport or a hotel that you have arrived □ *We checked in early and walked around the airport.*
□ *I checked in at a small hotel on the village square.*

check out

to pay the bill at a hotel and leave □ *They checked out yesterday morning.*

check up on someone or something

to find out information about a person or thing □ *I'm sure he knew I was checking up on him.*

cheer [tʃɪəʳ]

cheers	3rd person present
cheering	present participle
cheered	past tense & past participle

TRANSITIVE AND INTRANSITIVE to shout loudly to show that you are pleased or to encourage someone

Ⓘ *We cheered as she went up the steps to the stage.*

Ⓣ *Swiss fans cheered Jacob Hlasek during yesterday's match.*

PHRASAL VERB

cheer up or cheer someone up

to become happier or make someone feel happier □ *Cheer up. Life could be worse.*
□ *A trip to the movies would cheer you up.*

chicken [ˈtʃɪkɪn]

chickens	3rd person present
chickening	present participle
chickened	past tense & past participle

PHRASAL VERB

chicken out

to not do something because you are afraid *(informal)* □ *I wanted to ask Mom but I chickened out.*

chill [tʃɪl]

chills	3rd person present
chilling	present participle
chilled	past tense & past participle

TRANSITIVE to make something cold
□ *Chill the fruit salad in the fridge.*

chill out

to relax (informal) □ After school, we chill out and watch TV.

choose ✪ [tʃuz]

chooses	3rd person present
choosing	present participle
chose	past tense
chosen	past participle

TRANSITIVE AND INTRANSITIVE

1 to decide to have a person or thing
Ⓣ Each group will choose its own leader.
Ⓘ You can choose from several different patterns.

2 to do something because you want to
Ⓣ Many people choose to eat meat at dinner only.
Ⓘ You can remain silent if you choose.

chop [tʃɑp]

chops	3rd person present
chopping	present participle
chopped	past tense & past participle

TRANSITIVE to cut something into pieces with a knife □ He was chopping onions in the kitchen.

chop something down

to cut through the trunk of a tree with an ax □ Sometimes they chop down a tree for firewood.

chop something off

to remove something using scissors or a knife □ She chopped off all her golden hair.

chop something up

to chop something into small pieces
□ ...chopped up banana

clean [klin]

cleans	3rd person present
cleaning	present participle
cleaned	past tense & past participle

TRANSITIVE to remove the dirt from something □ He fell from a ladder while he was cleaning the windows.

clean something up

1 to clean objects or dirt away from a place □ Who is going to clean up this mess?
2 to clean a place completely □ While I'm out, could you clean up the kitchen?

clear [kliˤr]

clears	3rd person present
clearing	present participle
cleared	past tense & past participle

1 TRANSITIVE to remove things from a place because you do not want or need them there □ Can someone clear the table, please?

2 INTRANSITIVE When the sky clears, it stops raining. □ The sky cleared and the sun came out.

clear away or clear something away

to put the things that you have been using back in their proper place
□ The waitress cleared away the plates.
□ He helped to clear away after dinner.

clear something out

to clean up a space, and to throw away the things in it that you no longer want
□ I cleared out my desk before I left.

clear up

to make a place clean and neat □ The children played while I cleared up in the kitchen.

cling ✪ [klɪŋ]

clings	3rd person present
clinging	present participle
clung	past tense & past participle

INTRANSITIVE to hold someone or something tightly □ The man was rescued as he clung to the boat.

close [klouz]

closes	3rd person present
closing	present participle
closed	past tense & past participle

1 TRANSITIVE AND INTRANSITIVE to shut a door or a window, or to be shut

Ⓣ *If you are cold, close the window.*
Ⓘ *The door closed quietly behind him.*

2 INTRANSITIVE If a store closes, it stops being open, so that people cannot come and buy things. □ *The shop closes on Sundays and public holidays.*

PHRASAL VERB

close down or close something down

to stop all work in a place, usually for ever □ *That shop closed down years ago.* □ *The Government has closed down two newspapers.*

come ✪ [kʌm]

comes	3rd person present
coming	present participle
came	past tense
come	past participle

INTRANSITIVE

1 to arrive somewhere, or move toward someone □ *Two police officers came into the hall.* □ *Eleanor has come to see you.*

2 to happen □ *The announcement came after a meeting at the White House.*

3 come from something used for saying that someone or something started in a particular place □ *Nearly half the students come from other countries.* □ *Most of Germany's oil comes from the North Sea.*

4 come true used when something that you wish for or dream actually happens □ *My life-long dream has just come true.*

5 where someone is coming from You can use expressions like **I know where you're coming from** or **you can see where she's coming from** to say that you understand or agree with someone. □ *Do you see where I'm coming from?*

PHRASAL VERBS

come about

to happen □ *This situation came about when he gave up his job.*

come across someone or something

to find someone or something, or meet them by chance □ *I came across a photo of my grandparents when I was looking for my diary.*

come along

1 to go with you somewhere □ *I asked if she would come along to one of our meetings.*

2 to develop or progress □ *How's your research coming along?*

come back

to return to a place □ *He wants to come back to Montana.*

come down

1 to fall to the ground □ *The rain came down for hours.*

2 to become less than before □ *Interest rates should come down.*

come in

to enter a place □ *Come in and sit down.*

come off

to be removed □ *This lid won't come off.*

come on

used for encouraging someone to do something or to be quicker □ *Come on, or we'll be late.*

come out

When the sun comes out, it appears in the sky because the clouds have moved away. □ *Oh, look! The sun's coming out!*

come to something

to add up to a particular amount □ *Lunch came to $80.*

come up

1 to be mentioned in a conversation □ *The subject came up at work.*

2 When the sun comes up, it rises. □ *It will be great to watch the sun coming up.*

cool [kul]

cools	3rd person present
cooling	present participle
cooled	past tense & past participle

TRANSITIVE AND INTRANSITIVE to become lower in temperature, or to allow something to do this

I Drain the meat and allow it to cool.
T They use air conditioning to cool the air inside their homes.

PHRASAL VERB

cool down

1 to become lower in temperature
□ Once it cools down, you'll be able to touch it.
2 to become less angry □ He has had time to cool down now.

cost ✪ [kɑst]

costs	3rd person present
costing	present participle
cost	past tense & past participle

TRANSITIVE to have as a price □ This course costs $150 per person. □ It cost us over $100,000 to buy new equipment last year.

could

➡ See Key Verb entry on p. 140

count [kaʊnt]

counts	3rd person present
counting	present participle
counted	past tense & past participle

1 INTRANSITIVE to say all the numbers in order □ Nancy counted slowly to five.
2 TRANSITIVE to see how many there are in a group □ I counted the money.
□ I counted 34 sheep on the hillside.
3 INTRANSITIVE to be important □ Every penny counts if you want to be a millionaire.

PHRASAL VERB

count on someone or something

to feel sure that someone or something will help you □ You can count on us to keep your secret. □ Can we count on your support?

creep ✪ [krip]

creeps	3rd person present
creeping	present participle
crept	past tense & past participle

INTRANSITIVE to move somewhere quietly and slowly □ He crept up the stairs.

cross [krɑs]

crosses	3rd person present
crossing	present participle
crossed	past tense & past participle

TRANSITIVE AND INTRANSITIVE

1 to move to the other side of a place
T She crossed the road without looking.
I She stood up and crossed to the door.
2 to put one of your arms, legs or fingers on top of the other □ Jill crossed her legs.

PHRASAL VERB

cross something out

to draw a line through words □ He crossed out her name and added his own.

cry [kraɪ]

cries	3rd person present
crying	present participle
cried	past tense & past participle

1 INTRANSITIVE to have tears coming from your eyes □ I hung up the phone and started to cry.
2 TRANSITIVE to say something very loudly □ "Nancy Drew," she cried, "you're under arrest!"

PHRASAL VERB

cry out

to call out loudly because you are frightened, unhappy or in pain □ He was crying out in pain when the ambulance arrived.

curl [kɜrl]

curls	3rd person present
curling	present participle
curled	past tense & past participle

TRANSITIVE AND INTRANSITIVE to form curved shapes, or to make something do this
I Her hair curled around her shoulders.
T Maria curled her hair for the party.

PHRASAL VERB

curl up

to move your head, arms and legs close to your body □ She curled up next to him.

cut ✪ [kʌt]

cuts	3rd person present
cutting	present participle
cut	past tense & past participle

TRANSITIVE

1 to use something sharp to remove part of something, or to break it □ *Mrs. Haines cut the ribbon.*

2 to accidentally injure yourself on a sharp object so that you bleed □ *I started to cry because I cut my finger.*

3 to reduce something □ *We need to cut costs.*

PHRASAL VERBS

cut back on something
to reduce something □ *The school has cut back on spending.*

cut down on something
to use or do less of something □ *He cut down on coffee.*

cut something down
to cut through a tree so that it falls to the ground □ *They cut down several trees.*

cut something off
to remove something using scissors or a knife □ *Mrs. Johnson cut off a large piece of meat.*

cut something out
to remove something from what surrounds it using scissors or a knife □ *I cut the picture out and stuck it on my wall.*

cut something up
to cut something into several pieces □ *Cut up the tomatoes.*

dare
➡ See *KeyVerb* entry on p. 150

deal ✪ [diəl]

deals	3rd person present
dealing	present participle
dealt	past tense & past participle

TRANSITIVE to give playing cards to the players in a game of cards □ *She dealt each player a card.*

PHRASAL VERBS

deal in something
to buy or sell a particular type of goods □ *They deal in antiques.*

deal with someone or something
1 to give your attention to someone or something □ *Could you deal with this customer, please?*

2 to do what is necessary to achieve the result you want □ *How do you deal with an uninvited guest?*

3 to be concerned with a particular subject □ *The first part of the book deals with his early life.*

die [dai]

dies	3rd person present
dying	present participle
died	past tense & past participle

INTRANSITIVE to stop living □ *His friend died in a car accident.*

PHRASAL VERBS

die down
to become less strong □ *The wind died down.*

die out
to become less common and eventually disappear □ *How did the dinosaurs die out?*

dig ✪ [dɪg]

digs	3rd person present
digging	present participle
dug	past tense & past participle

TRANSITIVE AND INTRANSITIVE to make a hole in the ground

Ⓘ *I took the shovel and started digging.*

Ⓣ *First, he dug a large hole in the ground.*

PHRASAL VERBS

dig someone or something out
to get someone or something out by digging □ *After the earthquake, rescuers had to dig people out.*

dig something out
to discover something after it has been stored, hidden or forgotten for a long time □ *She dug out a photograph from under a pile of papers.*

dare [dɛ³r] and need [niːd]

MODAL VERBS

The verbs **dare** and **need** are called semi-modals. This is because they sometimes behave like modal verbs and at other times like main verbs.

> *He dared to speak./He doesn't dare to speak.*
>   (= **dare** as a main verb)
> *He dare not speak.* (= **dare** as a modal verb)

Dare and *need* as modal verbs

As modal verbs, **dare** and **need** do not have a 3rd person singular inflection (that is, they do not add **-s** to the form that goes with **he**, **she**, and **it**) and they are followed by the base form of a main verb. These verbs are mainly used in negatives and questions.

> *You needn't hurry.*
> *Dare I ask how the project's going?*

As a modal verb, **dare** has these forms:

> I **dare** not go.   I **dared** not go.
> He **dare** not go.   He **dared** not go.
> **Dare** he do it?
> **Dare** I do it?

The past form **dared** is rarely used as a modal verb.

Modal verb uses of *dare*

1 **Dare** is used in negative statements and questions to talk about taking risks, or about having enough courage to do something. In negative statements, you put ***dare not*** between the subject and the base form of the main verb. The contracted form ***daren't*** exists but it is almost never heard in American English.

> *Dare she risk staying where she was?*
> *I dare not tell him the truth. He'll go crazy.*

2 **Dare** is used for talking about courage or risk in positive statements in which there is a word with negative meaning in the same clause. This word can be outside the verb phrase, and may be a word with a negative sense, like ***only*** or ***never***.

> *No sensible driver dare risk driving in these conditions.*

3 You use **dare** for making suggestions or asking questions, especially when people may not like your suggestion or your question. These are often fixed expressions.

> *Dare I suggest that we do our homework now?*
> *Dare I ask where you have been?*

As a modal verb, **need** has these forms:

> ***Need*** *I go?* I ***need*** *not go.*
> ***Need*** *he go? He* ***need*** *not go.*
> ***Needn't*** *he go? He* ***needn't*** *go.*

The past form ***needed*** is not used as a modal verb.

Modal verb uses of *need*

1 **Need** is used in negative statements to tell someone not
to do something, or to advise or suggest that they do not do
something. Here, you put **need not** (or **needn't**) between the
subject and the base form of the main verb.

> *Please, you needn't shout.*
> *She need not know I'm here.*

2 **Need** is used in negative statements to tell someone that
something is not necessary, in order to make them feel better.
Here, you put **need not** (or **needn't**) between the subject and
the base form of the main verb.

> *You needn't worry. Everything is fine.*
> *You needn't come if you're busy.*

3 **Need** is used in negative statements to give someone permission
not to do something. Here you put **need not** (or **needn't**)
between the subject and the base form of the main verb.

> *You needn't come if you don't want to.*
> *He needn't talk about it if he doesn't want to.*

4 **Need** is used for talking about necessity in positive statements
in which there is a word of negative meaning in the same
clause. This word can be outside the verb phrase and may
be a word with a negative sense, such as **never** or **hardly**.

> *You're among friends now. You need never feel lonely again.*

5 You use **need** in fixed expressions, usually in the form of
questions, to show that the person you are talking to already
knows what you are going to say. Here you put the subject
between **need** and the base form of the main verb.

> *"What are you going to do today?"—"Need you ask?"*
> *"He was tall, dark and handsome. Need I go on?"*

Main verb uses of *dare* and *need*

As main verbs, **dare** and **need** have a 3rd person singular inflection (that is, they add -**s** to the form that goes with *he*, *she*, and *it*) and they are followed by the *to* infinitive. They can also use the auxiliary *do* and all the tenses that are appropriate to a main verb.

As a main verb, **dare** has these forms:

I **dare** to do it.	I **do not dare** to do it.
He **dares** to do it.	He **does not dare** to do it.
Does he **dare** to do it?	**Doesn't** he **dare** to do it?

Main verb senses of *dare*

1 If you **dare** to do something, you do something that needs a lot of courage.

> *Most people hate Harry but they don't dare to say so.*
> *She didn't dare to tell me where she'd been.*

2 If you **dare** someone to do something, you challenge them to do something to prove that they are not frightened to do it, or that they can do it even though it is difficult.

> *I dare you to watch that horror movie with all the lights out.*
> *He dared me to get through the whole speech without cracking up.*

As a main verb, **need** has these forms:

I **need** it.	I **need to do** it.
He **needs** it.	He **needs to do** it.
I **do** not **need** it.	I **do** not **need to do** it.

*He **does** not **need** it.*   *He **does** not **need** to **do** it.*
***Does** he **need** it?*   ***Does** he **need** to **do** it?*

Main verb senses of *need*

1 **Need** is used in negative statements to tell someone not to do something, or to advise or suggest that they do not do something. Here you put **do** + **not need** between the subject and the infinitive form of the main verb.

> *You don't need to apologize.*

2 **Need** is used in negative statements to tell someone that something is not necessary, in order to make them feel better. Here you put **do** + **not need** between the subject and the infinitive form of the main verb.

> *You don't need to worry. Everything's fine.*

3 **Need** is used in negative statements to give someone permission not to do something. Here you put **do** + **not need** between the subject and the infinitive form of the main verb.

> *You don't need to wait for me.*

Note that, with both **dare** and **need**, both the modal verb and the main verb often have the same meaning.

> *Anna **dared not jump** off the high fence.*
> *Anna **didn't dare to jump** off the high fence.*
> *You **needn't come** if you don't want to.*
> *You **don't need to come** if you don't want to.*

Phrase

how dare you/he/she/they?
You say **how dare you/he/she/they?** when you want to show
that you are very angry about something that someone has
done.

> *How dare you say that about my mother?*
> *How dare they barge in here while we're quietly eating
>   our dinner?*

dispose [dɪsˈpəʊz]

disposes	3rd person present
disposing	present participle
disposed	past tense & past participle

PHRASAL VERB

dispose of something

to get rid of something □ *How did they dispose of the body?*

divide [dɪˈvaɪd]

divides	3rd person present
dividing	present participle
divided	past tense & past participle

TRANSITIVE AND INTRANSITIVE

1 to separate something into smaller parts, or to separate in this way
Ⓣ *The class was divided into two groups of six.*
Ⓘ *Half a mile upstream, the river divides.*

2 to find out how many times one number can fit into another bigger number □ *Measure the floor area and divide it by six.*

3 to form a line that separates two areas □ *A border divides Mexico from the United States.*

4 to cause disagreement between people □ *Several major issues divided the country.*

PHRASAL VERB

divide something up

to separate something into smaller parts □ *They divided the country up into four areas.*

do

➡ See *Key Verb* entry on p. 158

doze [dəʊz]

dozes	3rd person present
dozing	present participle
dozed	past tense & past participle

INTRANSITIVE to sleep lightly or for a short period □ *She dozed for a while in the cabin.*

PHRASAL VERB

doze off

to start to sleep lightly □ *I closed my eyes and dozed off.*

draw ✪ [drɔː]

draws	3rd person present
drawing	present participle
drew	past tense
drawn	past participle

1 TRANSITIVE AND INTRANSITIVE to use a pencil or a pen to make a picture
Ⓘ *She was drawing with a pencil.*
Ⓣ *I've drawn a picture of you.*

2 INTRANSITIVE to attract □ *The case drew record interest for a business dispute before the supreme court.*

3 TRANSITIVE to move someone or something somewhere □ *He drew his chair nearer the fire.* □ *He drew Caroline close to him.*

4 INTRANSITIVE to finish a game with the same number of points as the other player or team □ *We drew 2–2 last weekend.*

5 draw to an end or close to end
□ *The party was drawing to a close.*
□ *I became aware that summer was drawing to an end.*

6 draw the curtains to pull the curtains across a window □ *He went to the window and drew the curtains.*

PHRASAL VERBS

draw something out

to take money out of a bank account, so that you can use it □ *A few months ago he drew out nearly all his money.*

draw something up

to write or type a list or a plan □ *They finally drew up an agreement.*

dream ✪ [driːm]

dreams	3rd person present
dreaming	present participle
dreamed,	past tense & past participle
dreamt	

INTRANSITIVE

1 to see events in your mind while you are asleep □ *Alma dreamt about her mother and father.*

2 to think about something that you would very much like to happen or have □ *She dreamed of becoming an actress.*

PHRASAL VERB

dream something up

to have an idea □ *I dreamed up a plan to solve both problems.*

dress [drɛs]

dresses	3rd person present
dressing	present participle
dressed	past tense & past participle

TRANSITIVE AND INTRANSITIVE to put clothes on yourself or someone else

Ⓘ *Sarah dressed quickly.*

Ⓣ *I washed and dressed the children.*

PHRASAL VERB

dress up

1 to put on formal clothes □ *You do not need to dress up for dinner.*

2 to put on clothes that make you look like someone else, for fun □ *He dressed up as a cowboy for the Halloween party.*

drift [drɪft]

drifts	3rd person present
drifting	present participle
drifted	past tense & past participle

INTRANSITIVE to be carried by the wind or by water □ *We drifted up the river.*

PHRASAL VERB

drift off

to gradually start to sleep □ *I finally drifted off just after midnight.*

drink ✪ [drɪŋk]

drinks	3rd person present
drinking	present participle
drank	past tense
drunk	past participle

1 TRANSITIVE AND INTRANSITIVE to take liquid into your mouth and swallow it

Ⓣ *He drank his coffee and left.*

Ⓘ *He ran to the pool of water and drank.*

2 INTRANSITIVE to drink alcohol □ *He drinks once a week.*

PHRASAL VERB

drink up or drink something up

to finish a drink completely □ *Drink up,*

there's time for another. □ *Drink up your soda and we'll go.*

drive ✪ [draɪv]

drives	3rd person present
driving	present participle
drove	past tense
driven	past participle

TRANSITIVE AND INTRANSITIVE

1 to control the movement and direction of a car or another vehicle

Ⓘ *She has never learned to drive.*

Ⓣ *We drove the car to Boston.*

2 to take someone somewhere in a car □ *She has always driven the children to school.*

drop [drɑp]

drops	3rd person present
dropping	present participle
dropped	past tense & past participle

> **Drop** or **fall**? Note that you cannot say that someone "falls" something. However, you can say that they **drop** something. *Leaves were falling to the ground… He dropped his phone.* If someone **falls** it is usually because of an accident. *He stumbled and fell.*

1 INTRANSITIVE to quickly become less in level or amount □ *Temperatures can drop to freezing at night.*

2 TRANSITIVE to let something fall □ *I dropped my glasses and broke them.*

3 TRANSITIVE to take someone somewhere in a car and leave them there □ *He dropped me outside the hotel.*

4 drop a hint to say what you are thinking in an indirect way □ *He has dropped hints that he is going to ask me to marry him.*

PHRASAL VERBS

drop by

to visit someone informally □ *She will drop by later.*

drop in

to visit someone informally □ *Why not drop in for a chat?*

do [duː]

AUXILIARY AND IRREGULAR VERB

does	3rd person present
doing	present participle
did	past tense
done	past participle

Do is an auxiliary verb and a main verb. You use the auxiliary form **do** or **did** with a main verb to make negatives and questions. As an auxiliary verb, **do** is not used with modal verbs.

I **do** not want it.	We **do** not want it.
You **do** not want it.	You **do** not want it.
He **does** not want it.	They **do** not want it.

I **did** not want it.	We **did** not want it.
You **did** not want it.	You **did** not want it.
He **did** not want it.	They **did** not want it.

Contracted forms

The positive forms of **do** cannot be contracted. In spoken English, the negative has these contracted forms.

I **don't** want it	We **don't** want it.
You **don't** want it.	You **don't** want it.
He **doesn't** want it.	They **don't** want it.

I **didn't** want it.	We **didn't** want it.
You **didn't** want it.	You **didn't** want it.
He **didn't** want it.	They **didn't** want it.

Auxiliary verb uses of *do*

The main uses of **do** as an auxiliary verb are to make negative forms and commands, questions, and to add emphasis.

1 **Do** is used for making the negative forms of present simple and past simple tenses. You put *not* between **do** and the base form of the main verb.

> *They do not want to work.*
> *I didn't feed the cat this morning.*
> *Jane arrived late but it didn't matter.*

2 **Do** is used for making the negative form of a command.

> *Don't shout!*
> *Don't run!*

3 **Do** is used for forming questions. You put the subject of the sentence after **do** and before the base form of the main verb.

> *Do you know what time it is?*
> *Where does she live?*
> *Did Tim say when he would arrive?*

4 **Do** is used in sentence tags, which come at the end of statements to make them into a kind of question. In negative question tags, you use the contracted negative form of **do**.

> *You know Andy, don't you?*
> *They went there on vacation last year, didn't they?*
> *You don't speak Italian, do you?*
> *You didn't see me, did you?*

5 **Do** is used for making the main verb stronger.

> *Veronica, I do understand what you're saying.*
> *I did lock the door; I know I did.*

6 **Do** is used for giving a short answer to a question. It is used alone in the answer; the main verb is not repeated.

> *"Do you think he is telling the truth?"—"Yes, I do."*
> *"Did you see Anne at the party?"—"No, I didn't."*
> *Jim likes jazz, I think.—Yes, he does.*

7 **Do** is used as a polite way of inviting or persuading someone to do something.

> *Do sit down.*
> *Do help yourself to another drink.*
> *Do let me see it!*

8 **Do** is used after *so* and *nor* to say that the same thing is true for two people or groups.

> *You know that's not true, and so do I.*
> *We didn't see what happened. Nor did John.*

9 You use **do** when you are comparing two people, things, or groups.

> *I earn more money than he does.*
> *One day, he'll leave us, just as his own father did.*

Do is also a main verb. You can use the main verb **do** to form negatives and questions by using **do** twice: once as an auxiliary verb and once as a main verb.

> *What does he do for a living?*
> *"Do I do it this way?"—"No, you don't do it like that at all."*
> *"Did you do your homework yesterday?"—"No, I didn't do it.*
> *   I forgot."*
> *Didn't Channa do the laundry?*

As a main verb, **do** can be used with modal verbs.

> *They will do it for you, if you ask them.*
> *I can do it, but I really shouldn't do it.*

Main verb senses of *do*

1 **Do** is used instead of a more specific verb. **Do** has many meanings including *carry out, perform, fix*, or *provide*.

> *I was trying to do some work.*
> *After lunch Elizabeth and I did the dishes.*

2 **Do** is used for talking about someone's job.

> *"What does your father do?"—"He's a doctor."*

3 **Do** is used for talking about habits.

> *What do you do over the weekend?*
> *I have always done it this way.*

4 **Do** is used for talking about behavior.

> *What is he doing?*
> *I did a really stupid thing the other day.*

5 **Do** is used for talking about plans.

> *What are you doing tonight?*

6 **Do** is used for talking about the subjects you study in a school or college.

> *I'd like to do physics in college.*
> *She did a course in acupuncture last year.*

7 **Do** is used for saying that something is good enough.

> *Can I please have something to eat? Anything will do.*

8 **Do** is used for saying that someone is successful or unsuccessful.

> *Connie did well in the debate.*
> *He did very badly in his chemistry exam.*

Phrasal verbs

do away with someone
to kill someone *(informal)*
Her husband tried to do away with her.

do away with something
to get rid of something
They want to do away with using paper.

do someone in
1 to kill someone *(informal)*
   They say his wife did him in.
2 to make someone extremely tired; to exhaust someone
   Replanting all the flower beds just about did me in.

do someone out of something
to prevent someone from getting something they expected to have *(informal)*
He feels I did him out of a job.

do someone over
to hurt someone badly
Let's get someone to do him over!

do something over
to do something again from the beginning; to repeat something
They'd like the chance to do it over.

do something up
1 to fasten something
   Marie did up the buttons on her jacket.
2 to decorate a room or building
   He has bought a new house and he's doing it up in Art Deco style.

do with something
to make good use of something; to benefit by having something
I could do with a glass of iced tea.
Can you do with those markers or should I get better ones?

do without something
to be able to continue although you do not have something
We can do without their help. We'll manage.

drop off

to start to sleep *(informal)* □ *Jimmy dropped off and started to snore.*

drop out

to stop attending school, or taking part in a competition, before you have finished □ *He dropped out of high school at the age of 16.*

drop someone off

to stop so that someone can get out of your car at a particular place □ *Dad dropped me off at school on his way to work.*

dry [draɪ]

dries	3rd person present
drying	present participle
dried	past tense & past participle

1 INTRANSITIVE to become dry □ *Let your hair dry naturally if possible.*

2 TRANSITIVE to remove the water from something □ *Mrs. Mason picked up a towel and began drying dishes.*

PHRASAL VERB

dry up

to become completely dry □ *The river dried up.*

eat ✪ [it]

eats	3rd person present
eating	present participle
ate	past tense
eaten	past participle

TRANSITIVE AND INTRANSITIVE to put something into your mouth and swallow it

Ⓣ *What did you eat last night?*

Ⓘ *I ate slowly and without speaking.*

Ⓘ *I was hungry because I hadn't eaten yet.*

PHRASAL VERB

eat something up

1 to eat all of something □ *Eat up that bit of salad, it won't keep.*

2 to receive or experience something enthusiastically □ *He performed his repertoire of "soft" hip-hop and the ladies in the crowd ate it up.*

end [ɛnd]

ends	3rd person present
ending	present participle
ended	past tense & past participle

TRANSITIVE AND INTRANSITIVE to reach the final point and stop, or to cause something to stop

Ⓘ *The meeting quickly ended.*

Ⓣ *She began to cry. That ended our discussion.*

PHRASAL VERB

end up

to be in a particular place or situation after a series of events □ *We ended up back at the house again.*

fall ✪ [fɑl]

falls	3rd person present
falling	present participle
fell	past tense
fallen	past participle

See note at **drop**.

INTRANSITIVE

1 to move quickly toward the ground by accident □ *Tyler fell from his horse and broke his arm.*

2 When rain or snow falls, it comes down from the sky. □ *More than 30 inches of rain has fallen in 6 days.*

3 to become less or lower □ *Here, temperatures at night can fall very quickly.*

4 fall asleep to start to sleep □ *He fell asleep in front of the fire.*

5 fall ill to become ill □ *Emily suddenly fell ill and was rushed to the hospital.*

PHRASAL VERBS

fall apart

to break into pieces □ *Gradually, the old building fell apart.*

fall behind

to fail to make progress or move forward as fast as other people □ *Some of the students fell behind in their work.*

fall down

to move quickly toward the ground by accident □ *The wind hit Chris so hard, he fell down.*

fall off or fall off something

to separate from something □ *His right shoe fell off but he kept on running.* □ *An engine fell off the wing of the airplane.*

fall out

to come out □ *His first tooth fell out when he was six.*

fall out with someone

to have an argument with someone and stop being friendly with them □ *Ashley has fallen out with her boyfriend.*

fall over

to move quickly toward the ground by accident □ *I fell over and broke my wrist.*

fall over something

to hit your foot on something and fall to the ground □ *She fell over her son's bike.*

fall through

to fail to happen as arranged □ *My house sale fell through.*

feed ✪ [fid]

feeds	3rd person present
feeding	present participle
fed	past tense & past participle

TRANSITIVE to give food to a person or an animal □ *It's time to feed the baby.* □ *She fed the dog a treat.*

feel ✪ [fil]

feels	3rd person present
feeling	present participle
felt	past tense & past participle

1 LINKING VERB to experience a particular emotion or physical feeling □ *I am feeling really happy today.*

2 LINKING VERB used for describing the way that something seems when you touch it or experience it □ *The blanket feels soft.*

3 TRANSITIVE to touch something with your hand, so that you can find out what it is like □ *The doctor felt my forehead.*

4 TRANSITIVE to be aware of something because you touch it or it touches you □ *Anna felt something touching her face.*

5 INTRANSITIVE to have an opinion about something □ *We feel that this decision is fair.*

6 feel like doing something to want to do something □ *"I just don't feel like going out tonight," Rose said quietly.*

PHRASAL VERBS

feel for someone

to have sympathy for someone □ *Nicole was crying, and I really felt for her.*

feel for something

to try to find something using your hands rather than your eyes □ *I felt for my wallet.*

fight ✪ [fait]

fights	3rd person present
fighting	present participle
fought	past tense & past participle

1 TRANSITIVE AND INTRANSITIVE to try to hurt someone by using physical force
I *"Stop fighting!" Mom shouted.*
T *"If we don't fight them, they will kill us!" he shouted.*

2 INTRANSITIVE to take part in a war □ *He fought in the war and was taken prisoner.*

3 TRANSITIVE to try very hard to stop something unpleasant □ *It is very hard to fight forest fires.*

4 INTRANSITIVE to try very hard to get something □ *Lee had to fight hard for his place on the team.*

5 INTRANSITIVE to argue *(informal)* □ *Robert's parents fight all the time.*

PHRASAL VERBS

fight back

to defend yourself by taking action against someone who has attacked you □ *The boys ran away when we fought back.*

fight someone off

to succeed in driving away someone who has attacked you □ *The man fought off his attacker.*

fight something back

to try very hard not to feel, show or act on an emotion □ *She fought back the tears.*

fight something off

to succeed in getting rid of an illness or an unpleasant feeling □ *He fought off the fear that was building inside him.*

figure ['fɪgjʊr]

figures	3rd person present
figuring	present participle
figured	past tense & past participle

1 TRANSITIVE to think or guess that something is the truth *(informal)* □ *I figured that's what she wanted.*

2 INTRANSITIVE to appear in something or to be included in it □ *Marriage doesn't figure in their plans.*

PHRASAL VERB

figure something out

to succeed in solving a problem *(informal)* □ *His parents could not figure out how to start their new computer.*

fill [fɪl]

fills	3rd person present
filling	present participle
filled	past tense & past participle

TRANSITIVE

1 to cause a container to become full of something □ *Rachel went to the bathroom and filled a glass with water.*

2 to cause a space to be full of something □ *Rows of desks filled the office.*

3 to put a substance into a hole to make the surface smooth □ *Fill the cracks between walls and window frames.*

PHRASAL VERBS

fill something in

1 to fill a hole to make a surface smooth □ *Start by filling in any cracks.*

2 to write information in the spaces on a form □ *When you have filled in the form, send it to your employer.*

fill something out

to write information in the spaces on

a form □ *Fill out the form, and keep a copy of it.*

fill up or **fill something up**

to become full or to make a container or an area full □ *The room was already starting to fill up as I arrived.* □ *Pass me your cup and I'll fill it up for you.*

find ✪ [faɪnd]

finds	3rd person present
finding	present participle
found	past tense & past participle

TRANSITIVE

1 to get something □ *David has finally found a job.*

2 to see or discover something, often after looking for it □ *I finally found my purse under the desk.*

3 used for expressing your opinion about something □ *I find his behavior extremely rude.* □ *We all found the play very funny.*

4 find someone guilty or not guilty to say that someone is guilty or not guilty of a crime □ *The woman was found guilty of fraud.*

5 find your way to get somewhere by choosing the right way to go □ *We lost our dog, but he found his way home.*

PHRASAL VERB

find something out

to learn the facts about something □ *I'll watch the next episode to find out what happens.*

finish ['fɪnɪʃ]

finishes	3rd person present
finishing	present participle
finished	past tense & past participle

1 TRANSITIVE to stop doing something □ *Dad finished eating and left the room.*

2 INTRANSITIVE to end □ *The concert finished just after midnight.*

PHRASAL VERB

finish something off

to eat or drink the last part of something

□ He took the bottle from her hands and finished it off.

fit [fɪt]

fits	3rd person present
fitting	present participle
fit	past tense & past participle
fitted	past tense & past participle

TRANSITIVE AND INTRANSITIVE

1 to be the right size for someone or something

Ⓣ *The costume fit the child perfectly.*

Ⓘ *The game is small enough to fit into your pocket.*

2 to attach something somewhere

□ *He fitted locks on the doors.*

PHRASAL VERBS

fit in

to be comfortable in a group because you are similar to other people in it □ *It's hard to see how he would fit in here.*

fit someone or something in

to find time or space for someone or something □ *We can't fit any more children in the car.* □ *The doctor can fit you in at 5 p.m.*

fling ✪ [flɪŋ]

flings	3rd person present
flinging	present participle
flung	past tense & past participle

TRANSITIVE to throw something somewhere using a lot of force □ *Kate flung the magazine across the table.*

fly ✪ [flaɪ]

flies	3rd person present
flying	present participle
flew	past tense
flown	past participle

1 INTRANSITIVE to move through the air □ *Once in the air, the bird flies at 40 mph.*

2 INTRANSITIVE to travel somewhere in an aircraft □ *We've flown to Los Angeles many times.*

3 TRANSITIVE AND INTRANSITIVE to make an aircraft move through the air

Ⓣ *He flew a small plane to Cuba.*

Ⓘ *I learned to fly in Vietnam.*

fold [fould]

folds	3rd person present
folding	present participle
folded	past tense & past participle

TRANSITIVE

1 to bend a piece of paper or cloth so that one part covers another part □ *He folded the paper carefully.*

2 fold your arms to put one arm under the other and hold them over your chest □ *He sat back and folded his arms across his chest.*

PHRASAL VERB

fold up or fold something up

to make something smaller by bending or closing parts of it, or to be able to be made smaller in this way □ *When you don't need to use it, the table folds up.* □ *Fold the ironing board up so that it is flat.*

follow ['fɒləʊ]

follows	3rd person present
following	present participle
followed	past tense & past participle

TRANSITIVE AND INTRANSITIVE

1 to move along behind someone

Ⓣ *We followed him up the steps.*

Ⓘ *They took him into a small room and I followed.*

2 to go to join someone who has gone somewhere □ *He followed Janice to New York.*

3 to happen or come after an event, activity or period of time

Ⓣ *...the days following Daddy's death.*

Ⓘ *He was arrested in the confusion that followed.*

4 as follows used for introducing a list or an explanation □ *The winners are as follows: E. Walker; R. Foster; R. Gates.*

PHRASAL VERBS

follow something through

to continue doing an action or plan until it is completed □ *I trained as an actress but I didn't follow it through.*

follow something up

to try to find out more about something, or to take action □ *A police officer took my statement, but no one has followed it up.*

fool [ful]

fools	3rd person present
fooling	present participle
fooled	past tense & past participle

TRANSITIVE to make someone believe something that is not true □ *Harris fooled people into believing she was a doctor.*

PHRASAL VERB

fool around

to behave in a silly way □ *They fool around and get into trouble at school.*

forbid ✪ [fər'bɪd, fɔr'bɪd]

forbids	3rd person present
forbidding	present participle
forbade	past tense
forbidden	past participle

TRANSITIVE to tell someone that they must not do something □ *My parents have forbidden me to see my boyfriend.* □ *His father forbade him from becoming a painter.*

forecast ✪ ['fɔrkæst]

forecasts	3rd person present
forecasting	present participle
forecast	past tense
forecast	past participle

TRANSITIVE to say what you think is going to happen in the future □ *Economists have forecast higher oil prices.* □ *More showers are forecast for this weekend.*

forget ✪ [fər'gɛt, fɔr'gɛt]

forgets	3rd person present
forgetting	present participle
forgot	past tense
forgotten	past participle

TRANSITIVE AND INTRANSITIVE

1 to not remember something
T *He never forgets his dad's birthday.*
I *I meant to lock the door, but I forgot.*

2 to not bring something with you
□ *When we reached the airport, I realized I'd forgotten my passport.*

3 to deliberately put something out of your mind □ *You will soon forget the bad experience you had today.*

forgive ✪ [fər'gɪv, fɔr'gɪv]

forgives	3rd person present
forgiving	present participle
forgave	past tense
forgiven	past participle

TRANSITIVE to stop being angry with someone who has done something bad or wrong □ *Hopefully Jane will understand and forgive you.* □ *Irene forgave Terry for stealing her money.* □ *I've never forgiven Peter for what he did.*

freak [frik]

freaks	3rd person present
freaking	present participle
freaked	past tense & past participle

PHRASAL VERB

freak out or **freak someone out**

to suddenly feel extremely surprised, upset, angry, or confused, or to cause people to feel this way □ *The first time I went onstage, I freaked out completely.* □ *I think our music freaks people out sometimes.*

freeze ✪ [friz]

freezes	3rd person present
freezing	present participle
froze	past tense
frozen	past participle

1 INTRANSITIVE to become solid because the temperature is low □ *If the temperature drops below 0°C, water freezes.*

2 TRANSITIVE AND INTRANSITIVE to make food or drink very cold in order to preserve it, or to be made cold in this way
T *You can freeze the soup at this stage.*
I *Most fresh herbs will freeze successfully.*

3 INTRANSITIVE to stand completely still □ *"Freeze!" shouted the police officer.*

freshen ['frɛʃən]

freshens	3rd person present
freshening	present participle
freshened	past tense & past participle

TRANSITIVE to make something look, smell, or feel cleaner and newer □ *This is a simple way to clean and freshen normal skin.*

PHRASAL VERB

freshen up

to wash your hands and face and make yourself look neat and clean □ *After Martine had freshened up, they went for a long walk.*

fuss [fʌs]

fusses	3rd person present
fussing	present participle
fussed	past tense & past participle

INTRANSITIVE to worry or behave in a nervous, anxious way about things that are not important □ *Carol said there was no need for anyone to fuss.*

PHRASAL VERB

fuss over someone

to pay someone a lot of attention and do things to make them happy or comfortable □ *Aunt Laura fussed over him all afternoon.*

get ✪ [gɛt]

gets	3rd person present
getting	present participle
got	past tense & past participle
gotten	past participle

> **Gotten** is an American form of the past participle that is used for all senses below. It is *not* used with **have got** when it means the same thing as **have**.

1 LINKING VERB to become □ *The boys were getting bored.*

2 TRANSITIVE to make or cause someone to do something □ *They got him to give them a lift in his car.*

3 TRANSITIVE to arrange for someone to do something for you □ *Why don't you get your car fixed?*

4 INTRANSITIVE to arrive somewhere □ *How do I get to your place from here?*

5 TRANSITIVE to buy or obtain something □ *Dad needs to get a birthday present for Mom.*

6 TRANSITIVE to receive something □ *I'm getting a bike for my birthday.*

7 TRANSITIVE to go and bring someone or something to a particular place □ *It's time to get the kids from school.*

8 TRANSITIVE to understand something □ *Dad laughed, but I didn't get the joke.*

9 TRANSITIVE to become ill with an illness or a disease □ *I got flu while I was in Spain.*

10 TRANSITIVE to leave a place on a particular train, bus, aeroplane, or boat □ *I got the train home at 10:45 pm.*

PHRASAL VERBS

get along with someone

to have a friendly relationship with someone □ *He's always complaining. I can't get along with him.*

get around

to move or travel from place to place □ *Rail travel through France is the perfect way to get around.*

get around

If news gets around, it is told to lots of people. □ *Word got around that he had been arrested.*

get around to something

to finally do something that you have been too busy to do □ *I haven't gotten around to talking to him yet.* □ *He hasn't gotten around to calling his mother.*

get away

to escape □ *The thieves got away through an upstairs window.*

get away with something

to not be punished for doing something wrong □ *The criminals drove off fast and got away with it.*

get back

to return somewhere □ *I'll call you when we get back from San Diego.*

get back to something
to return to a previous state or level □ *I couldn't get back to sleep.*

get by
to have just enough of something □ *We have enough money to get by.*

get down
to make your body lower until you are sitting, resting on your knees, or lying on the ground □ *Everybody got down on the ground when they heard the shots.*

get in
to reach a station or an airport □ *Our flight got in two hours late.*

get into something
to climb into a car □ *We said goodbye and I got into the taxi.*

get off something
to leave a bus, train, or bicycle □ *He got off the bus at Halsted Street.*

get on something
to enter a train or bus or sit on a bicycle □ *She got on the train just before it left.*

get on with someone Same as get along with someone in entry get

get on with something
to continue doing or to start doing something □ *It's time for you all to get on with the work now.*

get out of something
1 to leave a place because you want to escape from it □ *They got out of the country just in time.*
2 to leave a car □ *A man got out of the car and ran away.*

get over something
to become happy or well again after an unhappy experience or an illness □ *It took me a long time to get over her death.*

get through something
to complete a task or an amount of work □ *We got through plenty of work today.*

get together
to meet in order to talk about something or to spend time together □ *Christmas is a time for families to get together.*

get up
1 to move your body so that you are standing □ *I got up and walked over to the window.*
2 to get out of bed □ *They have to get up early in the morning.*

give ✪ [gɪv]

gives	3rd person present
giving	present participle
gave	past tense
given	past participle

TRANSITIVE

1 to let someone have something □ *My parents gave me a watch for my birthday.*
2 to pass an object to someone, so that they can take it □ *She'd given him a pillow and a blanket.*
3 used with nouns when you are talking about actions or sounds. For example, "She gave a smile" means "She smiled." □ *She gave me a big kiss.*

PHRASAL VERBS

give in
to agree to do something although you do not really want to do it □ *After saying "no" a hundred times, I finally gave in and said "yes."*

give something away
to give something that you own to someone □ *She likes to give away plants from her garden.*

give something back
to return something to the person who gave it to you □ *I gave the book back to him.*

give something out
to give one of a number of things to each person in a group □ *Our teacher gave out calculators for the math test.*

give something up
to stop doing or having something □ *We gave up hope of finding the fishermen.*

give up
to decide that you cannot do something and stop trying to do it □ *I give up. I'll never understand this.*

go ✪ [gou]

goes	3rd person present
going	present participle
went	past tense
gone	past participle

1 TRANSITIVE AND INTRANSITIVE to move or travel somewhere

Ⓘ *We went to Rome on vacation.*

Ⓣ *I went home for the weekend.*

2 INTRANSITIVE to leave the place where you are □ *It's time for me to go.*

3 INTRANSITIVE to leave a place in order to do something □ *We went swimming early this morning.* □ *He had gone for a walk.*

4 INTRANSITIVE to visit school, work or church regularly □ *Does your daughter go to school yet?*

5 INTRANSITIVE to lead to a place □ *This road goes from Randallstown to Frederick.*

6 INTRANSITIVE used for describing where you usually keep something □ *The shoes go on the shoe shelf.*

7 LINKING VERB to become □ *I'm going crazy.*

8 INTRANSITIVE used for talking about the way that something happens □ *How's your job going?* □ *Everything is going wrong.*

9 INTRANSITIVE to be working □ *Can you get my car going again?*

10 to go If you say that there is a certain amount of time **to go**, you mean that there is that amount of time left before something happens or ends. □ *There is a week to go until election day.*

PHRASAL VERBS

go ahead
to take place □ *The wedding went ahead as planned.*

go away
1 to leave a place or a person □ *Just go away and leave me alone!*

2 to leave a place and spend time somewhere else, especially as a vacation □ *Why don't we go away this weekend?*

go back
to return somewhere □ *He'll be going back to college soon.*

go by
to pass □ *The week went by so quickly.*

go down
1 to become less □ *House prices went down last month.*

2 When the sun goes down, it goes below the line between the land and the sky. □ *It gets cold after the sun goes down.*

go off
to explode □ *A bomb went off, destroying the car.*

go off someone or something
to stop liking someone or something (informal) □ *I started to go off the idea.*

go on
1 to continue to do something □ *She just went on laughing.*

2 to be happening □ *While this conversation was going on, I just listened.*

go out
1 to leave your home to do something enjoyable □ *I'm going out tonight.*

2 to stop shining or burning □ *The fire went out and the room became cold.*

go out with someone
to have a romantic relationship with someone □ *I've been going out with my girlfriend for three months.*

go over something
to look at something or think about it very carefully □ *We went over the details again.*

go through something
to experience something difficult □ *He went through a difficult time when his wife died.*

go together
to look or taste good together □ *Cheese and tomatoes go together well.*

go up
to become greater □ *The cost of calls went up to $1.00 a minute.*

go with something

to look or taste good with something else □ *Those slacks would go with my blue shirt.*

go without something

to not have or get something that you need □ *The soldiers had to go without food for days.*

grind ✪ [graind]

grinds	3rd person present
grinding	present participle
ground	past tense & past participle

TRANSITIVE to rub a substance against something hard until it becomes a fine powder □ *Grind some pepper into the sauce.* □ *...freshly ground coffee.*

grow ✪ [grou]

grows	3rd person present
growing	present participle
grew	past tense
grown	past participle

1 INTRANSITIVE to gradually become bigger □ *All children grow at different rates.*

2 INTRANSITIVE If a plant or a tree grows in a particular place, it lives there. □ *There were roses growing by the side of the door.*

3 TRANSITIVE to put seeds or young plants in the ground and take care of them □ *I always grow a few red onions.*

4 INTRANSITIVE to gradually become longer □ *My hair grows really fast.*

5 LINKING VERB to gradually change □ *He's growing old.*

PHRASAL VERBS

grow into something

to get bigger so that a piece of clothing fits properly □ *It's a bit big, but she'll soon grow into it.*

grow out of something

1 to stop behaving in a particular way as you get older □ *Most children who bite their nails grow out of it.*

2 to become too big to wear a piece of clothing □ *You've grown out of your shoes again.*

grow up

to gradually change from being a child into being an adult □ *She grew up in Tokyo.*

> **Grow up** or **bring up**? **Grow up** is an intransitive verb, and means to change from being a child to being an adult. *I grew up in southern Texas.* **Bring up** is a transitive verb, and means to look after a child. *Ellicott City is the perfect place to bring up a family.*

had better

➡ See *Key Verb* entry on pp. 243–245

hand [hænd]

hands	3rd person present
handing	present participle
handed	past tense & past participle

TRANSITIVE to put something into someone's hand □ *He handed me a piece of paper.*

PHRASAL VERBS

hand something in

to take something to someone and give it to them □ *I need to hand in my homework today.*

hand something out

to give one thing to each person in a group □ *My job was to hand out the prizes.*

hand something over

to give something to someone □ *The bank has been ordered to hand over financial records about pastor J. Scott Moore.*

hang ✪ [hæŋ]

hangs	3rd person present
hanging	present participle
hung, hanged	past tense & past participle

> The form **hung** is used as the past tense and past participle. The form **hanged** is used as the past tense and past participle for meaning **3**.

1 INTRANSITIVE to be attached to something without touching the ground □ *Flags hang at every entrance.*

2 **TRANSITIVE** to attach something somewhere so that it does not touch the ground □ *She hung her clothes outside to dry.*

3 **TRANSITIVE** to kill someone by tying a rope around their neck □ *The five men were hanged on Tuesday.*

PHRASAL VERBS

hang on
to wait *(informal)* □ *Can you hang on for a minute?*

hang on or hang onto something
to hold something very tightly □ *I closed my eyes and hung on tight.* □ *He hung onto the rail as he went downstairs.*

hang out
to spend a lot of time somewhere *(informal)* □ *I often hang out at the mall.*

hang up or hang up on someone
to end a phone call □ *Just as I was about to hang up, she answered.* □ *Don't hang up on me!*

have
➡ See *Key Verb* entry on p. 174

have got to
➡ See *Key Verb* entry on p. 179

have to
➡ See *Key Verb* entry on p. 182

hear [hiᵊr]

hears	3rd person present
hearing	present participle
heard	past tense & past participle

TRANSITIVE AND INTRANSITIVE

1 to be aware of a sound through your ears

T *She could hear music in the distance.*

I *He doesn't hear very well.*

2 to find out about something by someone telling you, or from the radio or television

I *My mother heard about the school from Karen.*

T *Have you heard the news?*

3 **hear from someone** to receive a letter, an email, or a telephone call from someone □ *It's always great to hear from you.*

4 **to have never heard of someone or something** to not know anything about someone or something □ *I don't know the man's face and I've never heard of his name.*

5 **someone won't or wouldn't hear of something** used for saying that someone refuses to let someone do something □ *They told me I needed to change but I wouldn't hear of it.*

PHRASAL VERB

hear of someone or something
to know about someone or something □ *I've heard of him, but I've never met him.*

heat [hit]

heats	3rd person present
heating	present participle
heated	past tense & past participle

TRANSITIVE to raise the temperature of something □ *Heat the tomatoes and oil in a pan.*

PHRASAL VERB

heat up or heat something up
to gradually become hotter or make something hotter □ *What will happen if the world heats up?* □ *Freda heated up some leftovers for me.*

help [hɛlp]

helps	3rd person present
helping	present participle
helped	past tense & past participle

TRANSITIVE AND INTRANSITIVE

1 to make it easier for someone to do something

T *Can someone help me, please?*

I *You can help by giving them some money.*

2 to improve a situation

I *Thanks for your advice. That helps.*

T *You can save money and help the environment.*

have [həv, strong hæv]

AUXILIARY AND IRREGULAR VERB

has	3rd person present
having	present participle
had	past tense
had	past participle

Have is an auxiliary verb and a main verb. As an auxiliary verb, you use **have** to form the perfect forms of main verbs. As a main verb, **have** has many different senses covering possession, appearance, position, and obligation.

As an auxiliary

I **have** read it.   We **have** read it.
You **have** read it.   You **have** read it.
He **has** read it.   They **have** read it.

I **had** read it.   We **had** read it.
You **had** read it.   You **had** read it.
He **had** read it.   They **had** read it.

As a main verb

I **have** it.   We **have** it.
You **have** it.   You **have** it.
He **has** it.   They **have** it.

I **had** it.   We **had** it.
You **had** it.   You **had** it.
He **had** it.   They **had** it.

Note that when **have** is a main verb it makes perfect forms like all other main verbs. This means that **have** can appear twice in present or past perfect sentences: once as an auxiliary verb and once as a main verb.

> We **have had** enough, thank you.
> They **had** already **had** several warnings.

Contracted forms

The present and past forms of **have** are often contracted in spoken English, especially when **have** is being used as an auxiliary verb.

> I/we/you/**they've** read it.
> He/**she's** read it.
> I/we/you/he/she/**they'd** read it.

Have as a main verb can also be contracted in spoken English, but this is not common in American English. Instead, the contracted form of the main verb is usually formed from **have got**.

> **I've got** a new car (not **I've** a new car).

Note that after certain modal verbs, the contracted form **'ve** sometimes sounds like **of**. Be careful not to make the mistake of writing, for example, **would of** instead of **would have**.

> She **would've** given you something to eat if you'd asked her.
> You **could've** stayed the night with us.

Making negatives

Have as an auxiliary verb
You make the negative of the auxiliary verb **have** by adding **not**

(or another negative word, such as **never**) immediately after it. There are three different negative forms you can use with **have**. If you use the full form **I have not**, you are emphasizing the negative aspect of a sentence. The form **I've not** is less strong and somewhat formal. The form **I haven't** is the most common of the three forms.

> **I/we/you/they have not** read it.
> **I/we/you/they've not** read it.
>
> **He/she has not** read it.
> **He/she's not** read it.
>
> **I/we/you/he/she/they had not** read it.
> **I/we/you/he/she/they'd not** read it.
>
> **I/we/you/they haven't** read it.
> **He/she hasn't** read it.
>
> **I/we/you/he/she/they hadn't** read it.
>
> Rachel **has never been** overseas before.
> She**'s not** told me about it yet.
> He **hasn't** found anywhere to stay.

As a main verb

You make the negative of the main verb **have** by putting the appropriate form of **do** + **not** (or **don't**) between the subject and **have**. You can also use **have not got** (or **haven't got**) as a negative form in the present tense.

> I/we/you/they **do not/don't have** it.
> He/she **does not/doesn't have** it.
> I/we/you/he/she/they **did not/didn't have** it.

I/we/you/they **haven't got** it.
He/she **hasn't got** it.
I/we/you/he/she/they **hadn't got** it.

She **doesn't have** any brothers or sisters.
I **haven't got** any idea what to do.
We **didn't have** enough money to pay for a taxi home.

In American English, the forms **had got(ten)** and **hadn't got(ten)** are used as perfect forms when *get* is the main verb, but not as past tense forms of *have got* when it means "possess."

I **haven't got** any idea what to do.
I **didn't have** any idea what to do. (not I **hadn't got** any idea what to do.)

Question forms

As an auxiliary verb

You make questions by putting the subject between the appropriate form of **have** and the past participle of the main verb.

Have you seen the car keys?
Had they been to Australia before?

As a main verb

You can make questions by using the appropriate form of *do* before the subject, followed by the appropriate form of **have**.

Do you have a pen?
Does she have my phone number?
Do you have time to see me now?

In older literature (for example, from the 19th century) you may see questions formed by simply putting the subject after the appropriate form of **have**. These forms are not used in modern American English, except in some fixed phrases such as *Have you* any idea . . . ?

> *Have you* a pen? (old-fashioned)
> *Have you* time to see me now? (old-fashioned)

Auxiliary verb uses of *have*

1 **Have** is used with a main verb to form the present or past perfect. You use the appropriate form of **have** (present or past), followed by the past participle.

> *Alex hasn't left yet.*
> *Matthew hasn't been feeling well today.*
> *I had already seen the movie.*

2 **Have** is used in sentence tags.

> *You haven't resigned, have you?*
> *He has apologized, hasn't he?*

3 **Have** is used for confirming or contradicting a statement containing *have*, *has* or *had*, or answering a question.

> *"Have you ever seen 'Titanic'?"—"No, I haven't."*
> *"Have you been to New York before?"—"Yes, we have."*

4 **Have** is used, with a past participle, to introduce a clause in which you mention an action that had already happened before another action began.

> *He arrived in Lodi at 2:30pm, having left San Francisco at 1pm.*

Main verb senses of *have*

1   You use **have** with a noun to talk about an action or event, when you could also use the same word as a verb.

> *She had a nap and changed her clothes./She napped and changed her clothes.*
> *Come and have a look at this!/Come and look at this!*

2   **Have** is used for saying that someone owns something. You cannot use continuous forms with this sense.

> *The children have lots of toys.*
> *He doesn't have any friends.*
> *Do you have any change?*

In spoken English, you can also use **have got** for this sense in the present tense. For the past tense, use **didn't have**, not **haven't got**.

> *She hasn't got any money.*
> *Has she got my phone number?*

3   **Have** is used for talking about people's relationships.

> *Do you have any brothers or sisters?*

4   **Have** is used for talking about a person's appearance or character.

> *You have beautiful eyes.*
> *She has a lot of courage.*

5   **Have** is used, instead of 'there is', to say that something exists or happens.

> *You have no choice.*
> *Jim has a fantastic view from his condo.*

6 **Have** is used for saying that someone has an illness or an injury.

> *I have a headache.*
> *Janet has a nasty cold.*
> *He has a broken leg.*

7 **Have** is used for saying that something, such as a part of your body, is in a particular position or state.

> *He had his hand on Anne's shoulder.*
> *They had the door closed so I couldn't hear.*

8 You use **have** for saying that you are responsible for doing something, or that you must do it. See also pp.182–184 **have to** and **have got to**.

> *I have an urgent phone call to make.*
> *Nick had lots of homework to do last night.*

Phrasal verbs

have at someone/something
to start to attack someone or something, or (with food), to start to eat it
I just put the pizza on the table. Have at it!
The reporters will have at her as soon as she steps out of the limo.

have it in for someone
to not like someone and to want to make life difficult for them
He's always had it in for me.

have anything/something on
to be busy because of a planned activity
Have you got anything on this evening?
I'll just look at my calendar and see if I have something on that weekend.

have something out with someone
to discuss a problem or a disagreement very openly with someone
because you think this is the best way to solve the problem
Why not have it out with her, discuss the whole thing face to face?

Phrase

have something done
If you have something done, someone does it for you, or you
arrange for someone to do it for you.
I had the windows cleaned yesterday.
You've had your hair cut; it looks great.

have got to [gɑt]

PHRASAL MODAL VERB

You use **have got to** for talking about obligation, necessity, and certainty in the same way that you use **have to** (p. 184). You use the appropriate form of **have** with **got to** and the base form of a main verb. **Have got to** is somewhat more informal, and often more emphatic, than **have to**.

> *I've got to clean the house before my cousins arrive.*
> *You have got to stop talking and listen to me.*
> *There has got to be an explanation for his strange behavior.*

Negative forms

Most speakers, rather than use the possible forms **have not got to/haven't got to**, use the negative forms of **have to**.

> *We do not have/We don't have to go to school tomorrow. It's a holiday.*

Past form

You do not use **have got to** with a past form. Use **have to** instead.

> *I had to work all weekend. (not **I had** got to work all weekend.)*

Question forms

> *Have you got to work this weekend?*
> *Haven't you got to work this weekend?*

Main senses

1   **Have got to** is used for saying that someone must do
something or that something must happen. Note that you do
not use **got** with the negative form.

>   *I'm not happy with the decision, but I've just got to accept it.*
>   *He's got to go home now.*
>   *They didn't have to pay tax.*

2   You use **have got to** for saying that you are certain that
something is true.

>   *You've got to be joking! You can't be serious.*
>   *There's got to be a solution to this problem.*

have to [həv, strong hæv]

PHRASAL MODAL VERB

You use **have to** for talking about obligation, necessity and certainty. You use the appropriate form of **have** with **to**, followed by the base form of a main verb. See also **have got to** (pp.182–183).

> *I have to go home soon.*
> *I will have to hurry to get there on time.*

Negative forms

To make the negative form, you use **do not have to**, followed by the base form of the main verb.

> *It's all right. You don't have to explain.*
> *It's very kind of you but you didn't have to do that.*

Question forms

> *Do you have to go already?*
> *Did you really have to say that?*

Main senses

1 **Have to** is used for saying that something is necessary, or that something must happen. If you **do not have to** do something, it is not necessary or required.

> *We'll have to find a taxi.*
> *He had to go to Dallas on business.*

2 You use **have to** for saying that you are certain that something is true or will happen.

> *There has to be a reason for this change of plans.*

3 can't help something to be unable to stop the way you feel or behave □ *I couldn't help laughing when I saw her face.*

4 help yourself to take what you want of something □ *There's bread on the table. Help yourself.*

help out or **help someone out**
to help someone by doing a job for them or giving them money □ *I'd like to help out but I honestly can't see what I could do.* □ *It cost a lot, and my mother had to help me out.*

hide ✪ [haid]

hides	3rd person present
hiding	present participle
hid	past tense
hidden	past participle

1 TRANSITIVE to put something or someone in a place where they cannot easily be seen or found □ *He hid the bicycle behind the wall.*

2 INTRANSITIVE to go somewhere where people cannot easily find you □ *The little boy had hidden in the wardrobe before.*

3 TRANSITIVE to cover something so that people cannot see it □ *She hid her face in her hands.*

4 TRANSITIVE to not let people know what you feel or know □ *Lee tried to hide his excitement.*

hit ✪ [hɪt]

hits	3rd person present
hitting	present participle
hit	past tense & past participle

TRANSITIVE

1 to touch someone or something with a lot of force □ *She hit the ball hard.*

2 to affect a person, place, or thing very badly □ *The earthquake hit northern Peru.*

3 hit it off to become friendly with someone as soon as you meet them (informal) □ *They didn't hit it off right away.*

hold ✪ [hould]

holds	3rd person present
holding	present participle
held	past tense & past participle

TRANSITIVE

1 to have something in your hands or your arms □ *She held his hand tightly.*

2 to put something into a particular position and keep it there □ *Try to hold the camera still.*

3 to be able to contain a particular amount of something □ *One CD-ROM disk can hold over 100,000 pages of text.*

4 to organize a particular activity such as a party or a meeting □ *The country will hold elections within a year.*

hold on or **hold onto something**
to keep your hand on or around something □ *You must hold on tightly. Don't fall!* □ *The thief pulled hard but I held onto my handbag.*

hold someone or **something back**
to stop someone or something from moving forward or from doing something □ *The police held back the crowd.*

hold someone up
to make someone late □ *I won't hold you up — I just have one quick question.*

hold something back
to not tell someone the full details about something □ *You seem to be holding something back.*

hold something out
to move your hand, or something that is in your hand toward someone □ *"I'm Nancy Drew," she said, holding out her hand.*

hunt [hʌnt]

hunts	3rd person present
hunting	present participle
hunted	past tense & past participle

TRANSITIVE AND INTRANSITIVE to chase and kill wild animals for food or as a sport

Ⓣ *He liked to hunt rabbits.*
Ⓘ *She hunts as often as she can.*

PHRASAL VERBS

hunt for someone or something

to search for someone or something
□ *He hunted for an apartment.*

hunt someone or something down

to succeed in finding someone or something after searching for them □ *It took her four months to hunt him down.*

hurry ['hʌri]

hurries	3rd person present
hurrying	present participle
hurried	past tense & past participle

INTRANSITIVE to move or do something as quickly as you can □ *Claire hurried along the road.* □ *Everyone hurried to find a seat.*

PHRASAL VERB

hurry up

to do something more quickly □ *Hurry up and get ready, or you'll miss the bus!*

hurt ✪ [hɜrt]

hurts	3rd person present
hurting	present participle
hurt	past tense & past participle

1 TRANSITIVE to make someone or something feel pain □ *I fell over and hurt my leg yesterday.*

2 INTRANSITIVE When part of your body hurts, you feel pain there □ *His arm hurt.*

3 TRANSITIVE to say or do something that makes someone unhappy □ *I'm really sorry if I hurt your feelings.*

join [dʒɔin]

joins	3rd person present
joining	present participle
joined	past tense & past participle

TRANSITIVE

1 to move or go to the same place as someone or something □ *His wife and children will join him in their new home next month.*

2 to become a member of an organization □ *He joined the Army five years ago.*

3 to meet or come together
Ⓣ *We stopped at the Summit rest stop where the old Lincoln highway joins I-80.*
Ⓘ *...Allahabad, where the Ganges and the Yamuna rivers join.*

4 to fasten, fix, or connect things together □ *'And' is often used to join two sentences.*

PHRASAL VERBS

join forces

to work together with someone to achieve something □ *Sutherland, along with other grieving mothers, joined forces earlier this year to form Belizeans for Justice.*

join in or join in something

to become involved in something that is happening □ *I wanted to join in but only two people could play.* □ *Thousands of people will join in the celebrations.*

jot [dʒɑt]

jots	3rd person present
jotting	present participle
jotted	past tense & past participle

PHRASAL VERB

jot something down

to write something down quickly □ *David jotted down the address on a notepad.*

keep ✪ [kip]

keeps	3rd person present
keeping	present participle
kept	past tense & past participle

1 LINKING VERB to remain in a particular state or place □ *We burned wood to keep warm.*

2 LINKING VERB to make someone or something stay in a particular state or place □ *He kept his head down, hiding his face.*

3 TRANSITIVE to continue to have something □ *I want to keep these clothes, and I want to give these away.*

4 **TRANSITIVE** to store something in a particular place □ *She kept her money under the bed.*

5 keep a promise to do what you said you would do □ *He kept his promise to come to my birthday party.*

6 keep doing something to do something many times or continue to do something □ *I keep forgetting the password for my computer.* □ *She kept running although she was exhausted.*

keep something up

to continue to do something □ *I could not keep the diet up for longer than a month.*

keep up with someone

to move as fast as another person so that you are moving together □ *Sam walked faster to keep up with his father.*

kick [kɪk]

kicks	3rd person present
kicking	present participle
kicked	past tense & past participle

TRANSITIVE AND INTRANSITIVE to move one or both your legs with quick, strong movements, once or repeatedly

T *The baby smiled and kicked her legs.*

I *They were dragged away shouting and kicking.*

kick someone out

to force someone to leave a place (informal) □ *He helped me after I was kicked out of art school.*

kneel ✪ [niːl]

kneels	3rd person present
kneeling	present participle
kneeled, knelt	past tense & past participle

INTRANSITIVE to bend your legs and rest with your knees on the ground □ *She knelt by the bed and prayed.*

kneel down

to rest on your knees □ *She kneeled down beside him.*

knock [nɑk]

knocks	3rd person present
knocking	present participle
knocked	past tense & past participle

1 **INTRANSITIVE** to hit something in order to make a noise □ *She went to Simon's place and knocked on the door.*

2 **TRANSITIVE** to touch or hit something roughly □ *She knocked the glass and it fell off the shelf.*

knock someone down

to injure or kill someone by driving into them □ *He died in the hospital after being knocked down by a car.*

knock someone out

to hit someone hard on the head so that they go into a sort of deep sleep □ *He was knocked out in a fight.*

knock someone or something over

to hit someone or something so that they fall to the ground □ *The third wave was so strong it knocked me over.*

knock something down

to destroy a building or part of a building □ *We're knocking down the wall between the kitchen and the dining room.*

know ✪ [nou]

knows	3rd person present
knowing	present participle
knew	past tense
known	past participle

TRANSITIVE AND INTRANSITIVE

1 to have a fact or an answer in your mind

T *You should know the answer to that question.*

I *"How old is he?" — "I don't know."*

2 to be familiar with a person or a place □ *I've known him for nine years.*

3 to understand something □ *I know*

how you feel.

4 I know used when you are agreeing with what someone has just said □ *"The weather is awful." — "I know."*

5 you know used when you want someone to listen to what you are saying (informal) □ *I'm doing this for you, you know.*

6 you never know used for saying that something is possible, although it is unlikely □ *I imagine he'll stay here but you never know.*

lay ✪ [lei]

lays	3rd person present
laying	present participle
laid	past tense & past participle

See note at **lie**.

TRANSITIVE

1 to put something somewhere carefully □ *He laid the newspaper on the desk.*

2 When a female bird lays an egg, it pushes an egg out of its body. □ *My pet canary has laid an egg.*

lead ✪ [lid]

leads	3rd person present
leading	present participle
led	past tense & past participle

1 TRANSITIVE to go in front of a group of people □ *A jazz band led the parade.*

2 TRANSITIVE to take someone to a place □ *I took his hand and led him into the house.*

3 INTRANSITIVE used for describing where a road or path goes □ *This path leads down to the beach.*

4 INTRANSITIVE to be winning in a race or competition □ *The Eagles led by three points at half-time.*

5 TRANSITIVE to be in control of a group of people □ *Chris leads a large team of salespeople.*

6 TRANSITIVE used for describing someone's life □ *She led a normal, happy life.*

PHRASAL VERB

lead to something

to cause a particular situation □ *Every*

time we talk about money it leads to an argument.

lean [lin]

leans	3rd person present
leaning	present participle
leaned	past tense & past participle

1 INTRANSITIVE to bend your body in a particular direction □ *They stopped to lean over a gate.*

2 TRANSITIVE AND INTRANSITIVE to rest against something so that it partly supports you, or to make something do this

Ⓘ *Lou was at the bus stop, leaning on her cane.*

Ⓣ *Lean your bike against the wall.*

PHRASAL VERB

lean toward something

to tend to think or act in a particular way □ *Politically, I lean toward the right.*

leap ✪ [lip]

leaps	3rd person present
leaping	present participle
leaped, leapt	past tense & past participle

INTRANSITIVE

1 to jump high in the air or a long distance □ *He leaped in the air and waved his hands.*

2 to move somewhere suddenly and quickly □ *The two men leapt into the car and drove away.*

learn [lɜrn]

learns	3rd person present
learning	present participle
learned	

TRANSITIVE AND INTRANSITIVE to get knowledge or a skill by studying, training, or through experience

Ⓣ *I learned Spanish in school.*

Ⓘ *Good teachers help you learn quickly.*

Ⓣ *He learned to play the piano at a very early age.*

leave ✪ [liv]

leaves	3rd person present
leaving	present participle
left	past tense & past participle

TRANSITIVE AND INTRANSITIVE

1 to go away from a place or person
🅣 *He left the country yesterday.*
🅘 *My flight leaves in less than an hour.*

2 to not bring something with you
□ *I left my bags in the car.*

3 to not use all of something □ *Please leave some cake for me!*

4 to give something to someone when you die □ *He left everything to his wife when he died.*

5 to forget to bring something with you
□ *I left my purse in the gas station.*

6 leave someone alone to stop annoying someone □ *Please just leave me alone!*

7 leave something alone to stop touching something □ *Leave my purse alone!*

PHRASAL VERBS

leave someone or something behind

to go away from someone or something permanently □ *When he went, he left behind a wife and two young children.*

leave someone or something out

to not include someone or something
□ *Why did they leave her out of the discussion?*

lend ✪ [lend]

lends	3rd person present
lending	present participle
lent	past tense & past participle

TRANSITIVE

1 to give someone money that they must give back after a certain amount of time □ *I lent him 20 bucks to take his kids to the movies.*

2 to allow someone to use something of yours for a period of time □ *Will you lend me your pen?*

let ✪ [let]

lets	3rd person present
letting	present participle
let	past tense & past participle

TRANSITIVE

1 to not try to stop something from happening □ *I just let him sleep.*

2 to give someone your permission to do something □ *I love marshmellows but Mom doesn't let me eat them very often.*

3 to allow someone to enter or leave a place □ *I went down and let them into the building.*

4 to allow someone to live in or use your property in exchange for money □ *The suite on the sixth floor has been let to a law firm.*

5 used when you are offering to do something □ *Let me hang up your coat.*

6 let go of someone or something to stop holding a thing or a person □ *She let go of Mona's hand.*

7 let's short for "let us"; used when you are making a suggestion □ *I'm bored. Let's go home.*

8 let someone know to tell someone about something □ *I want to let them know that I'm safe.*

PHRASAL VERBS

let someone down

to disappoint someone, usually by not doing something that you said you would do □ *Don't worry, Robert, I won't let you down.*

let someone off

1 to give someone a lighter punishment than they expect or no punishment at all □ *He thought that if he said he was sorry, the judge would let him off.*

2 to give someone permission not to do a job or duty □ *They let me off work to go to the wedding.*

let something down

to allow air to escape from something that is filled with air, such as a tire
□ *Someone had let the tires down on my car.*

let something in

to allow something such as air or water to get in or pass through □ *There is no glass in the front door to let light in.*

let something out

to allow something such as air or water to flow out or escape □ *It lets sunlight in but doesn't let heat out.*

lie ✪ [laɪ]

lies	3rd person present
lying	present participle
lay	past tense
lain	past participle

> **Lie** or **lay**? **Lie** does not have an object. *Lie on the floor with your arms by your sides.* **Lay** has an object. *Lay the baby on the bed.*

INTRANSITIVE

1 to be in a flat position, and not standing or sitting □ *I lay awake for hours, trying not to worry.*

2 to be in a flat position on a surface □ *Broken glass lay all over the carpet.*

PHRASAL VERBS

lie around

to be left somewhere in an untidy way □ *My dad had lots of old books lying around.*

lie down

to move your body so that it is flat on a surface, usually when you want to rest or sleep □ *Why don't you go upstairs and lie down?*

light ✪ [laɪt]

lights	3rd person present
lighting	present participle
lit, lighted	past tense & past participle

TRANSITIVE

1 to produce light for a place □ *The room was lit by only one light.*

2 to start something burning □ *Stephen took a match and lit the candle.*

lighten ['laɪtən]

lightens	3rd person present
lightening	present participle
lightened	past tense & past participle

TRANSITIVE AND INTRANSITIVE to make something less dark, or to become less dark

Ⓣ *She lightened her hair with a special cream.*

Ⓘ *It was 5:45 a.m. and the sky was beginning to lighten.*

PHRASAL VERB

lighten up

to start to be more relaxed and less serious □ *You should lighten up and enjoy yourself a bit more.*

line [laɪn]

lines	3rd person present
lining	present participle
lined	past tense & past participle

TRANSITIVE to form a row along the edge or side of something. □ *Thousands of local people lined the streets.* □ *...a long tree-lined drive.*

PHRASAL VERB

line up or **line something up**

to move to form a row or a line □ *The senior leaders lined up behind him in neat rows.* □ *The boy lined up his toys on the windowsill.*

link [lɪŋk]

links	3rd person present
linking	present participle
linked	past tense & past participle

TRANSITIVE

1 to form a logical relationship between two things □ *There's plenty of evidence to link smoking with an early death.*

2 to form a physical connection between two or more things □ *The Rama Road links the capital, Managua, with the Caribbean coast.*

3 to join things by putting part of one through the other □ *She linked her arm through his.*

PHRASAL VERB

link someone up

to connect two or more things □ *One day everyone will be linked up to broadband.*

live [lɪv]

lives	3rd person present
living	present participle
lived	past tense & past participle

> When you are talking about someone's home, the verb **live** has a different

meaning in the continuous form than it does in the simple tenses. For example, if you say "*I'm living in Washington*," this suggests that the situation is temporary and you may soon move to a different place. If you say "*I live in Washington*," this suggests that Washington is your permanent home.

1 INTRANSITIVE to have your home in a particular place □ *She lived in New York for ten years.*
2 TRANSITIVE to have a particular type of life □ *Pete lives a quiet life in Arkansas.*
3 INTRANSITIVE to be alive □ *We all need water to live.*
4 INTRANSITIVE to stay alive until you are a particular age □ *He lived to 103.* □ *My father died ten years ago, but he lived to see his first grandson.*

PHRASAL VERBS

live off someone
to rely on someone to provide you with money □ *He had lived off his father all his life.*

live off something
to have a particular amount of money to buy things □ *She had to live off $46 a week.*

live on something
1 to eat a particular type of food □ *Sheep live mainly on grass.*
2 to have a particular amount of money to buy things □ *Most students are unable to live on $9000 per year.*

live up to something
to achieve the thing that was expected □ *Sales have not lived up to expectations this year.*

lock [lɑk]

locks	3rd person present
locking	present participle
locked	past tense & past participle

TRANSITIVE
1 to close a door or a container with a key □ *Are you sure you locked the front door?*
2 to put a thing or a person somewhere

and to close the door or the lid with a key □ *She locked the case in the cupboard.*

PHRASAL VERBS

lock someone away
to put someone in prison or in a hospital for people who are mentally ill □ *People who commit serious crime should be locked away.*

lock someone in
to put someone in a room and lock the door so that they cannot get out □ *Manda shouted that Mr. Holt had no right to lock her in.*

lock someone out
to prevent someone from entering a room or building by locking the doors □ *They had a fight and she locked him out of the apartment.*

lock something away
to put something in a container and close it with a key □ *She cleaned her jewelry and locked it away in a case.*

lock up or lock something up
to lock all the windows and doors of a house or a car □ *Don't forget to lock up before you leave.* □ *He locked the house up and drove away.*

lock yourself out
to be unable to get into a room or building because you do not have your key □ *The new owners locked themselves out of their apartment.*

log [lɑg]

logs	3rd person present
logging	present participle
logged	past tense & past participle

TRANSITIVE to write something down as a record of an event □ *They log everything that comes in and out of the warehouse.*

PHRASAL VERBS

log in or log on
to type an identifier and a password so that you can start using a computer or a website □ *She turned on her computer and logged in.*

log off or log out

to stop using a computer or website by clicking on an instruction □ *I logged off and went out for a walk.*

look [lʊk]

looks	3rd person present
looking	present participle
looked	past tense & past participle

See note at **see**.

1 INTRANSITIVE to turn your eyes in a particular direction so that you can see what is there □ *I looked out of the window.*

2 INTRANSITIVE to try to find someone or something □ *We looked everywhere, but we couldn't find her.* □ *I'm looking for a child.*

3 INTRANSITIVE If you look at a situation or a thing, you examine it, consider it, or judge it. □ *My eye hurts; can you look at it?* □ *Next semester we'll look at the period before World War II.*

4 LINKING VERB to seem or appear □ *"You look lovely, Marcia!"*

5 look out used when you are warning someone that they are in danger □ *"Look out!" somebody shouted, as the semi started to roll toward us.*

PHRASAL VERBS

look after someone

to take care of someone □ *Maria looks after the kids while I'm at work.*

look after something

to deal with something because it is your responsibility □ *We'll help you look after your money.*

look around or look around something

to walk around a place and look at the different parts of it □ *Would you like to come in and look around?* □ *We went to look around the new houses.*

look back

to think about things that happened in the past □ *Looking back, I was pretty stupid.*

look down on someone

to consider someone to not be as good as you □ *I wasn't successful, so they looked down on me.*

look forward to something

to want something to happen because you think you will enjoy it □ *She's looking forward to her holiday in Hawaii.*

look into something

to find out about something □ *He had once looked into buying his own island.*

look on someone or something

to have a particular opinion of someone or something □ *Supporting the team, like paying local sales taxes, was looked on as a civic duty.*

look out for something

to pay attention so that you see something if it happens □ *Officers are looking out for the stolen car.*

look something up

to find a piece of information by looking in a book or on a computer □ *I looked up your number in my address book.*

look through something

to examine different parts of a book or magazine □ *Peter started looking through the mail.*

look up to someone

to respect and admire someone □ *Younger children look up to their parents and want to be like them.*

lose ☉ [luz]

loses	3rd person present
losing	present participle
lost	past tense & past participle

TRANSITIVE AND INTRANSITIVE

1 to not win a game
Ⓣ *Our team lost the game by one point.*
Ⓘ *No one likes to lose.*

2 to not know where something is □ *I've lost my keys.*

3 to not have something any more because someone has taken it away from you □ *I lost my job when the company shut down.*

4 lose money used when a business earns less money than it spends □ *The company has been losing money for the last three years.*

5 lose weight to become less heavy □ *His doctor told him to lose weight.*

make ☉ [meik]

makes	3rd person present
making	present participle
made	past tense & past participle

1 TRANSITIVE to produce, build, or create something □ *She makes all her own clothes.*

2 TRANSITIVE used with nouns to show that someone does or says something □ *I made a few phone calls.*

3 TRANSITIVE to cause someone to do or feel something □ *The smoke made him cough.*

4 TRANSITIVE to force someone to do something □ *Mom made me apologize to him.*

5 TRANSITIVE to earn money □ *He's good-looking, smart and makes lots of money.*

6 LINKING VERB to produce a particular total when added together □ *Two and two make four.*

7 make something into something to change something so that it becomes a different thing □ *They made their condo into a beautiful home.*

PHRASAL VERBS

make do or **make something do**

to manage with what is available □ *They tried to make do with only three plates and three bowls.* □ *It's not much money but we have to make it do.*

make someone or **something out**

to be able to see, hear or understand someone or something □ *I couldn't make out what he was saying.*

make something up

to invent something such as a story or excuse □ *It was all lies. I made it all up.*

make up

to become friends again after an argument □ *You two are always fighting and then making up again.*

make up for something

to provide something in the place of something that is lost or missing □ *The work is not great but the money you earn makes up for this.*

make up something

to be members or parts of a larger thing □ *Women officers make up 13 per cent of the police force.*

may

➡ See *Key Verb* entry on p. 192

mean ☉ [min]

means	3rd person present
meaning	present participle
meant	past tense & past participle

TRANSITIVE

1 to have a particular meaning □ *What does 'software' mean?*

2 used for saying that a second thing will happen because of a first thing □ *The new factory means more jobs for people.*

3 to be serious about what you are saying □ *He said he loves her, and I think he meant it.*

4 I mean used when you are explaining, justifying, or correcting what you have just said □ *It was his idea. Gordon's, I mean.* □ *I'm sure he wouldn't mind. I mean, I was the one who asked him.* □ *It was law or classics — I mean English or classics.*

5 mean a lot to someone to be very important to someone □ *Be careful with the photos. They mean a lot to me.*

6 mean to do something to do something deliberately □ *I'm so sorry. I didn't mean to hurt you.*

meet ☉ [mit]

meets	3rd person present
meeting	present participle
met	past tense & past participle

1 TRANSITIVE to see someone who you know by chance and speak to them □ *I met Shona in town today.*

may [meɪ] and might [maɪt]

MODAL VERBS

You use **may** and **might** to ask for and give permission, and when you are talking about possibility. **May** and **might** are used with the base form of the main verb.

Contracted forms

There is no contracted positive form of **may** or **might**.
The contracted negative form of **might** is **mightn't**. There is a contracted negative form of **may** — **mayn't** — that may be seen in older literature, but it is not used in modern American English.

> *I mightn't have enough time to call you this evening.*
> *We might come and live here, mightn't we?*

When you are changing sentences from direct to reported speech, **may** usually becomes *could*, though it is also acceptable to change it to *might*.

> *"May I come in?" Nicki asked.*
> *Nicki asked if she could come in.*
> *Nicki asked if she might come in.*

Main senses

1 **May** is used for asking permission in a more formal way than *can*.

May I have a drink, please?
May we come in?

Might is also used in this way but only in very formal situations.

Might I ask your name?

2 **May** is used, particularly with *you*, *he*, *she*, *they*, or a noun designating a person or group of people, to show that the speaker is giving permission for something to happen.

You may go now.
You may pay with cash or by credit card.
Users may download forms from this website.

3 Both **may** and **might** are used for talking about the possibility that something will happen or be true in the future. Using **might**, rather than **may**, shows that it is slightly less likely that something will happen or be true.

The weather may/might be better tomorrow.
This opportunity may/might not come again.
I may/might regret this decision.

4 Both **may** and **might** are used for talking about the possibility that something is true, although this is not certain. Using **might**, rather than **may**, shows that it is slightly less likely that something is true.

You may/might be right.
He may/might not be interested in her any more.

5 **May** is often used for politeness, to make an order appear as a request; **might** is used to make the speaker more distant from the request.

> *You may leave us now.*
> *You might want to put the TV volume down a little.*

6 You use **may** or **might** as a polite way of interrupting someone, asking a question, or introducing what you are going to say next.

> *May I just ask you one other thing?*
> *Might I make a suggestion?*
> *Might I trouble you for some more tea?*

7 Might is used in conditional sentences to show possibility. The *if* clause can be in either the present or the past tense. Compare with *could*; see p.143.

> *If Lucinda comes, she might take care of the children.*

2 **TRANSITIVE** to see someone who you do not know and speak to them for the first time □ *I have just met an amazing man.*

3 **INTRANSITIVE** to go somewhere with someone because you have planned to be there together □ *We could meet for a game of tennis after work.*

4 **TRANSITIVE** to go to a place and wait for someone to arrive □ *Mom met me at the airport.*

5 **INTRANSITIVE** to join together □ *This is the point where the two rivers meet.*

mess [mɛs]

messes	3rd person present
messing	present participle
messed	past tense & past participle

PHRASAL VERBS

mess about or mess around

to spend time doing things for fun, or for no particular reason □ *We were just messing around playing with paint.*

mess something up

1 to make something go wrong (*informal*) □ *This has messed up our plans.*

2 to make a place or a thing dirty or messy (*informal*) □ *He didn't want to mess up his hair.*

might

➡ See *Key Verb* entry on p. 194

miss [mɪs]

misses	3rd person present
missing	present participle
missed	past tense & past participle

TRANSITIVE AND INTRANSITIVE

1 to not manage to hit or catch something

Ⓣ *Morrison just missed the ball.*

Ⓘ *He threw the paper toward the bin, but missed.*

2 to not notice something □ *What did he say? I missed it.*

3 to feel sad that someone is not with you □ *I miss my family terribly.*

4 to feel sad because you no longer have something □ *I love my new apartment, but I miss my garden.*

5 to arrive too late to get on an airplane, train, boat, or bus □ *He missed the last bus home.*

6 to not take part in a meeting or an activity □ *He missed the party because he had to work.*

PHRASAL VERB

miss out on something

to not have the chance to take part in something □ *You missed out on all the fun yesterday.*

mistake ✪ [mɪˈsteɪk]

mistakes	3rd person present
mistaking	present participle
mistook	past tense
mistaken	past participle

TRANSITIVE

1 to wrongly think that one person is another person □ *People always mistook Lauren for her sister because they were so alike.* □ *She was often mistaken for a man.*

2 **there's no mistaking** You can say **there is no mistaking** something when you are emphasizing that you cannot fail to recognize or understand it. □ *There's no mistaking his voice.*

mix [mɪks]

mixes	3rd person present
mixing	present participle
mixed	past tense & past participle

1 **TRANSITIVE** to put different things together so that they make something new □ *Mix the sugar with the butter.*

2 **INTRANSITIVE** to join together and make something new □ *Oil and water don't mix.*

PHRASAL VERB

mix someone or something up

to think that one of two things or people is the other one □ *I mixed Jane up with someone else.*

move [muv]

moves	3rd person present
moving	present participle
moved	past tense & past participle

1 TRANSITIVE to put something in a different place □ *A police officer asked him to move my car.*

2 INTRANSITIVE to change position or go to a different place □ *The train began to move.*

3 INTRANSITIVE to go to live in a different place □ *She's moving to Utah next month.*

4 TRANSITIVE to make someone have strong feelings, especially of sadness, pity, or sympathy □ *The story surprised and moved me.*

PHRASAL VERBS

move around

to keep changing your job or keep changing the place where you live □ *I was born in Fort Worth but we moved around a lot after that.*

move in

to begin to live somewhere □ *A new family has moved in next door.*

move off

to start moving away □ *Gilbert waved his hand and the car moved off.*

move on

1 to leave the place where you have been, and go somewhere else □ *He wants to sell his land and move on.*

2 to finish or stop one activity and start doing something different □ *Now, can we move on and discuss something else?*

move out

to stop living in a particular place □ *I wasn't happy living there, so I decided to move out.*

move up or move something up

1 to change position to a better, higher, or more advantageous one □ *The price of gold moved up for the third day in a row.*

2 To bring closer to the present time □ *Qantas has moved up delivery of eight of its* 50 ordered Boeing 787 Dreamliners by around two years.

mow ✪ [mou]

mows	3rd person present
mowing	present participle
mowed	past tense & past participle
mown	past participle

TRANSITIVE to cut an area of grass using a machine called a mower □ *Connor was in the garden, mowing the lawn.* □ *...the smell of mown grass.* □ *Bill mowed lawns for neighbors.*

must

➡ See *Key Verb* entry on p. 199

need

➡ See *Key Verb* entry on p. 150

occur [ə'kɜr]

occurs	3rd person present
occurring	present participle
occurred	past tense & past participle

INTRANSITIVE to happen □ *The car crash occurred at night.*

PHRASAL VERB

occur to someone

to suddenly come into someone's mind □ *Suddenly it occurred to her that the door might be open.*

ought to

➡ See *Key Verb* entry on p. 203

part [part]

parts	3rd person present
parting	present participle
parted	past tense & past participle

PHRASAL VERB

part with something

to give or sell something that you would prefer to keep □ *Think carefully before parting with money.*

pass [pæs]

passes	3rd person present
passing	present participle
passed	past tense & past participle

must [məst, strong mʌst]

MODAL VERB

You use **must** for talking about obligation and necessity, and for giving orders and advice. For these meanings, it can only be used to refer to the present or the future. When referring to the past, you use a form of **have to** (see p.184). When you are changing sentences from direct to reported speech, you change **must** to **have to**.

> "I **must** write that letter this evening," said Janet.
> Janet said that she **had to** write a letter this evening.

Contracted forms

There is no contracted positive form of **must**. The contracted negative form of **must** is **mustn't**.

> You mustn't worry so much.

Making negatives

You use **must not** or **mustn't** to make negative statements. **Mustn't** comes between the subject and the main verb.

> He **must not** come in here.
> I **mustn't** forget to call Dad.

Main senses

1   **Must** is used for saying that something is very important or necessary. In positive sentences it is interchangeable in this sense with **have to**.

> *Some people will criticize you, but you must cope with this.*
> *We must not forget to send Tom a birthday card.*

2   **Must** is used for saying that it is necessary for something to happen, usually because of a rule or law.

> *All students must wear school uniforms.*
> *Drivers must stop at a red traffic light.*

3   **Must** is used for giving orders firmly and positively. It is interchangeable with **have to** in this sense.

> *You must go to sleep now.*
> *You must clean your room this morning.*

4   **Must** is used for giving advice or making strong recommendations.

> *You must talk to your lawyer.*
> *You really must see this movie. It's very funny.*

5   **Must** is used for expressing a firm intention to do something. It is interchangeable with **have to** in this sense.

> *I must be leaving.*
> *I must speak to Tanya at once.*

6   **Must** is used for showing that you are fairly sure that something is true, based on reason or the available evidence. When you are talking about the past, you use **must have** with the past participle of the main verb.

Claire's car isn't here so she must be at work.
He must have decided not to come.

7 **Must** is used in questions. Note that many speakers prefer to use **have to** instead.

Must you go so soon?
Do you have to go so soon?

Must not and **mustn't** are used in the following ways:

1 to forbid someone to do something.

You must not cross the road when the light is red.
You mustn't tell anyone about this.

2 to talk about an event or a state that is unacceptable.

There mustn't be any mistakes in your letter.
Whales must not become extinct.

Note that when you are expressing the fact that someone is not obliged to do something, you use **do not have to**. Compare:

*You **must not** come in here.*
    (= You do not have permission to come in here.)
*You **don't have to** come in here.*
    (= You are not obliged to come in here if you don't want to.)

Pass or **spend**? You can say that time **has passed** in order to show that a period of time has finished. *The first few days passed…* If you **spend** a period of time doing something, you do that thing for all of the time you are talking about. *I spent three days cleaning our flat.*

1 TRANSITIVE AND INTRANSITIVE to go past someone or something
Ⓣ *When she passed the library door, the telephone began to ring.*
Ⓘ *Jane stood aside to let her pass.*

2 INTRANSITIVE to move in a particular direction □ *A helicopter passed overhead.*

3 TRANSITIVE to give an object to someone □ *Pam passed the books to Dr. Wong.*

4 TRANSITIVE to kick or throw a ball to someone □ *Hawkins passed the ball to Payton.*

5 INTRANSITIVE to go by □ *Time passes quickly when you are enjoying yourself.*

6 TRANSITIVE to spend time in a particular way □ *The children passed the time watching TV.*

7 TRANSITIVE AND INTRANSITIVE to succeed in an examination
Ⓣ *Tina passed her driving test last week.*
Ⓘ *I'm afraid I didn't pass.*

8 TRANSITIVE to formally agree to a new law □ *The government passed a law that allowed banks to sell insurance.*

PHRASAL VERBS

pass away
to die □ *She passed away last year.*

pass out
to suddenly become unconscious
□ *He felt sick and then passed out.*

pass something around
to take something and then give it to another person in a group □ *The cookies were passed around.*

pass something on
to give someone some information
□ *Mary Hayes passed on the news to McEvoy.*

pass for someone
to be accepted as someone □ *In that uniform you could pass for a real cop.*

pass something up
to not take advantage of an opportunity
□ *We can't pass up a chance like this.*

pay ✪ [pei]

pays	3rd person present
paying	present participle
paid	past tense & past participle

See note at **buy**.

TRANSITIVE AND INTRANSITIVE

1 to give someone an amount of money for something such as a bill or something that you are buying
Ⓣ *She paid the hotel bill before she left.*
Ⓘ *You can pay by credit card.*

2 to give someone money for the work that they do □ *The lawyer was paid a huge amount.*

PHRASAL VERBS

pay off
to be successful and bring a good result
□ *All their hard work has finally paid off.*

pay someone back
1 to give someone the money that you owe them □ *He promised to pay the money back as soon as he could.*

2 to make someone suffer for something bad that they did to you □ *Some day I'll pay you back for this!*

phase [feiz]

phases	3rd person present
phasing	present participle
phased	past tense & past participle

TRANSITIVE to do something in stages
□ *The job cuts will be phased over two years.*

PHRASAL VERBS

phase something in
to introduce something gradually □ *The pay raise will be phased in over two years.*

phase something out
to gradually stop using or doing

ought to [ɑt]

PHRASAL MODAL VERB

Ought to is similar to **should** in meaning. Like **should**, **ought to** does not have a past form. See pp.220–221 for **should**.

Ought to is used in questions and negatives mainly by speakers of regional dialects. In negatives, you put **not** between **ought** and **to**. In questions, you put the subject between **ought** and **to**.

> *Ought we to do this without asking Dad's permission?*
> *I ought not to have said those things to her.*

Some speakers use a bare infinitive in negative sentences with **ought**:

> *Applying the same ethics to medical care ought not be that hard.*
> *He spoke only when the boy did things he thought children ought not do.*

Contracted forms

The contracted negative form of **ought** is **oughtn't (to)**.

> *We oughtn't to have done that.*
> *Well, if she's really sorry, she ought to apologize, oughtn't she?*

Main senses

1 You use **ought to** for saying that something is the right or sensible thing to do, especially when you are giving or asking

for advice or suggestions. Here you use **ought to** and the base form of the main verb.

> *You ought to hire a lawyer.*
> *People ought to be a bit more understanding.*

2 **Ought to** is used with ***have*** followed by the past participle to say that something was the right or sensible thing to do, but that someone did not do it. You use this form of **ought to** to show that you feel sorry that you did not do something, or to show that you are angry with someone else for not doing something.

> *I'm so sorry. I ought to have told you the truth.*
> *Ludovic ought to have phoned his parents.*

3 You use **ought to** for saying that you think that something will be true, or that something will happen. You use **ought to** and the base form of the main verb here.

> *"This party ought to be fun," said Alex.*
> *Annabel ought to be here soon.*

4 You use **ought to** for politely telling someone that you must do something, for example that you must leave.

> *I think I ought to go. It's getting late.*
> *I really ought to be leaving.*

5 **Ought to** is used in questions and negatives. People often use ***should*** instead of **ought to** here because it sounds more natural and less formal.

> *Ought I to report this incident to someone in authority?*
> *Should I report this incident to someone in authority?*
> *Ought we to make a start?*
> *Should we make a start?*

something □ *The old phone system is being phased out.*

pick [pɪk]

picks 3rd person present
picking present participle
picked past tense & past participle

TRANSITIVE

1 to choose a particular person or thing □ *Mr. Nowell picked ten people to interview.*
2 to take flowers, fruit, or leaves from a plant or tree □ *I've picked some flowers from the garden.*

pick on someone

to repeatedly criticize someone or treat them unkindly *(informal)* □ *Bullies often pick on younger children.*

pick someone or something out

1 to recognize someone or something when it is difficult to see them □ *I had trouble picking out the words, even with my glasses on.*
2 to choose someone or something from a group of people or things □ *They picked me out to represent the whole team.*

pick someone or something up

to collect someone or something from a place, often in a car □ *Could you please pick me up at 5 p.m?*

pick something up

1 to lift something up □ *He picked his cap up from the floor.*
2 to learn a skill or an idea over a period of time without really trying *(informal)* □ *Her children have picked up English really quickly.*
3 to get an illness from somewhere or something □ *Some passengers had picked up food poisoning.*

piece [pis]

pieces 3rd person present
piecing present participle
pieced past tense & past participle

piece something together

1 to gradually make something complete by joining its parts together □ *Doctors carefully pieced together the broken bones.*
2 to gradually discover the truth about something □ *Francis was able to piece together what had happened.*

pile [paiᵊl]

piles 3rd person present
piling present participle
piled past tense & past participle

TRANSITIVE to put things somewhere so that they form a pile □ *He was piling clothes into the suitcase.*

pile something up

to put one thing on top of another to form a pile □ *They piled up rocks to build a wall.*

pile up

to increase in number □ *Problems were piling up at work.*

pin [pɪn]

pins 3rd person present
pinning present participle
pinned past tense & past participle

TRANSITIVE

1 to fasten something with a pin □ *They pinned a notice to the door.*
2 to press someone firmly against something so that they cannot move □ *I pinned him against the wall.*
3 to say that someone is responsible for something bad □ *They couldn't pin the killing on anyone.*

pin someone down

to force someone to make a definite statement □ *She couldn't pin him down to a date.*

pin something down

to try to discover exactly what, where, or

when something is □ *It has taken a long time to pin down its exact location.*

plan [plæn]

plans	3rd person present
planning	present participle
planned	past tense & past participle

TRANSITIVE AND INTRANSITIVE to decide in detail what you are going to do

T *We were planning our holidays.*

T *He planned to leave Baghdad on Monday.*

I *We must plan for the future.*

PHRASAL VERB

plan on something

to intend to do something □ *They were planning on getting married.*

play [pleɪ]

plays	3rd person present
playing	present participle
played	past tense & past participle

1 INTRANSITIVE to spend time doing enjoyable things, such as using toys and taking part in games □ *Polly was playing with her teddy bear.*

2 TRANSITIVE AND INTRANSITIVE to take part in a sport, game, or match

T *Alain was playing cards with his friends.*

I *I want to play for my country.*

3 TRANSITIVE to compete against another person or team in a sport or game □ *Northern Ireland will play Latvia.*

4 TRANSITIVE to perform as a character in a play or film □ *His ambition is to play the part of Dracula.*

5 TRANSITIVE AND INTRANSITIVE to produce music from an instrument

T *Nina had been playing the piano.*

I *The orchestra played beautifully.*

6 TRANSITIVE to listen to something that has been recorded, such as a CD □ *She played her records too loudly.*

7 INTRANSITIVE If music plays, it is produced by a radio or CD player so that people can hear it. □ *Classical music was playing in the background.*

8 play a joke/trick on someone to deceive someone or give them a surprise for fun □ *She wanted to play a trick on her friends.*

PHRASAL VERBS

play around

to behave in a silly way to amuse yourself or other people *(informal)* □ *Stop playing around and eat!*

play something back

to listen to sounds or watch pictures after recording them □ *We played the phone message back several times, but we couldn't understand it.*

play something down

to try to make people think that something is less important than it really is □ *Managers played down reports that 10,000 jobs could be lost.*

play something up

to strongly emphasize or create a positive impression about something □ *Darrell and Michael Waltrip are the only brothers to each win a Daytona 500, and they played it up for the crowd.*

plug [plʌg]

plugs	3rd person present
plugging	present participle
plugged	past tense & past participle

TRANSITIVE to block a hole with something □ *We are working to plug a major oil leak.*

PHRASAL VERB

plug something in

to connect a piece of electrical equipment to the electricity supply □ *I had a TV, but there was no place to plug it in.*

point [pɔint]

points	3rd person present
pointing	present participle
pointed	past tense & past participle

1 INTRANSITIVE to use your finger to show where someone or something is □ *I pointed at the boy sitting near me.*

2 TRANSITIVE to hold a camera or a weapon toward someone or something □ *She smiled when Laura pointed a camera at her.* □ *The man was pointing a gun at my head.*

point something out

to tell someone about a fact or show it to them □ *He pointed out the mistakes in the book.*

pop [pɑp]

pops	3rd person present
popping	present participle
popped	past tense & past participle

1 INTRANSITIVE to make a short sharp sound □ *The cork popped and shot to the ceiling.*

2 TRANSITIVE to put something somewhere □ *He popped a chocolate into his mouth.*

3 INTRANSITIVE to go somewhere for a short time □ *He just popped into a clothing store to buy some flip-flops.*

pop up

to appear in a place or situation unexpectedly □ *You solve one problem and another immediately pops up.*

print [prɪnt]

prints	3rd person present
printing	present participle
printed	past tense & past participle

TRANSITIVE

1 to use a machine to put words or pictures on paper □ *The publishers have printed 40,000 copies of the novel.*

2 to write using letters that are not joined together □ *Please sign here, then print your name and address.*

print something out

to use a machine to produce a copy of a computer file on paper □ *I printed out a copy of the letter.*

pull [pʊl]

pulls	3rd person present
pulling	present participle
pulled	past tense & past participle

TRANSITIVE AND INTRANSITIVE to hold something firmly and use force to move it

T *I helped to pull the boy out of the water.*

I *Pull as hard as you can.*

pull away

When a vehicle pulls away, it starts moving forward. □ *I watched the car pull away.*

pull in

to stop a vehicle somewhere □ *The bus pulled in at the side of the road.*

pull into something

to move a vehicle into a place and stop there □ *David pulled into the driveway in front of her garage.*

pull out

to move a vehicle out into the road or nearer the center of the road □ *I looked in the rearview mirror, and pulled out into the street.*

pull over

to move a vehicle closer to the side of the road and stop there □ *I pulled over to let the police car pass.*

pull something down

to deliberately destroy a building □ *They pulled the offices down, leaving a large open space.*

pull something off

to manage to achieve something successfully □ *It will be amazing if they pull it off.*

pull through

to recover from a serious illness □ *We didn't know if he would pull through or not.*

pull up

to slow down a vehicle and stop □ *The taxi pulled up and the driver jumped out.*

pull yourself together

to control your feelings and be calm again □ *"Now stop crying and pull yourself together!"*

pump [pʌmp]

pumps	3rd person present
pumping	present participle
pumped	past tense & past participle

TRANSITIVE to make a liquid or a gas flow in a particular direction □ *The heart pumps blood around the body.*

PHRASAL VERB

pump something up

to fill something such as a tire with air □ *Pump all the tires up to the recommended pressure.*

push [pʊʃ]

pushes	3rd person present
pushing	present participle
pushed	past tense & past participle

TRANSITIVE AND INTRANSITIVE

1 to use force to make something move away from you or away from its previous position

Ⓣ *He pushed the door open.*

Ⓘ *He put both hands on the door and pushed.*

2 to use force in order to move past someone □ *He pushed his way toward her, laughing.*

3 to encourage or force someone to do something □ *James pushed her into stealing the money.*

4 to try to convince people to accept or buy something □ *Salespeople always try to push their products.*

PHRASAL VERBS

push ahead

to make progress □ *The government pushed ahead with building the airport.*

push in

to come into a line in front of other people □ *Nina pushed in next to Lisa.*

push on

to continue with a journey or task □ *Searching for treasure, Columbus pushed on to Cuba.*

push someone around

to give someone orders in a rude and insulting way □ *He came in with lots of money and tried to push people around.*

push someone or something over

to push someone or something so that they fall onto the ground □ *People have damaged hedges and pushed over walls.*

put ❂ [pʊt]

puts	3rd person present
putting	present participle
put	past tense & past participle

TRANSITIVE

1 to move something into a particular place or position □ *Steven put the photograph on the desk.*

2 to cause someone or something to be in a particular state or situation □ *Your carelessness put the children in danger.*

PHRASAL VERBS

put in something

to spend an amount of time or effort doing something □ *We put in three hours' work every evening.*

put someone off or put someone off something

to cause someone to dislike or disbelieve something □ *He was trying to put us off thinking everything will be alright.*

put someone out

to cause someone trouble or inconvenience □ *I'm sorry to put you out, but could you help me, please?*

put someone through

to connect someone on the telephone to the person they want to speak to □ *Hold on, please. I'll just put you through.*

put something away

to put something back in the place where it is usually kept □ *Kyle put the milk away in the fridge.*

put something back

to delay doing something □ *The trip has been put back to Easter.*

put something down

1 to stop holding something and place it

on a surface □ *The woman put down her newspaper and looked at me.*

2 to write or type something □ *Mr. Allen put down his thoughts on paper.*

put someone down

to say critical or negative things about someone □ *Before you start putting her down, you'd better be sure of your facts.*

put something off

to delay doing something □ *Tony always puts off making difficult decisions.*

put something on

1 to place clothing or make-up on your body □ *Grandma put her coat on and went out.*

2 to make a piece of electrical equipment start working □ *Maria sat up in bed and put on the light.*

3 to make recorded music start to play □ *I put some music on.*

put something out

1 to make a fire stop burning □ *All day, firefighters have been trying to put out the fire.*

2 to stop a light shining by pressing a switch □ *He crossed to the table and put out the light.*

3 to place things where they are ready to be used □ *I put the teapot out on the table.*

4 to move a part of your body forward □ *She put her hand out and touched her mother's arm.*

put something up

1 to build a wall or a building □ *The Smiths have put up electric fences on their farm.*

2 to attach a poster or a notice to a wall or board □ *They're putting new street signs up.*

put someone up

to provide accommodation for someone for a short time □ *Who's putting you up while you're in LA?*

put up with something

to accept someone or something

unpleasant without complaining □ *I won't put up with your bad behavior any longer.*

quit ✪ [kwɪt]

quits	3rd person present
quitting	present participle
quit	past tense & past participle

TRANSITIVE AND INTRANSITIVE

1 to choose to stop a job or other activity (informal)

Ⓣ *Christina quit her job last year.*

Ⓘ *That's enough! I quit!*

2 to stop doing something □ *Quit talking now and do some work.*

read ✪ [riːd]

reads	3rd person present
reading	present participle
read	past tense & past participle

> When it is the present tense, **read** is pronounced [riːd]; **read** is also the past tense and past participle when it is pronounced [red].

TRANSITIVE AND INTRANSITIVE

1 to look at written words and understand them

Ⓣ *Have you read this book?*

Ⓘ *She spends all her time reading.*

2 to say words that you can see □ *Kevin always read a story to the twins when he got home.*

PHRASAL VERBS

read something out

to read something to other people □ *She asked us to read out the answers to the exercise.*

read up on something

to inform yourself about a subject by reading □ *You will need to read up on how the market works.*

rid ✪ [rɪd]

rids	3rd person present
ridding	present participle
rid	past tense & past participle

TRANSITIVE to succeed in removing something unwanted completely □ *He tried to rid himself of these unpleasant thoughts.* □ *The Pied Piper had rid the town of rats.*

ride ✪ [raid]

rides	3rd person present
riding	present participle
rode	past tense
ridden	past participle

> When you want to say that someone is controlling a horse, bicycle, or motorbike, you use **ride** as a transitive verb: *They taught her how to ride a motorbike.* If **ride** is used without an object, preposition, or any other phrase, it usually refers to riding a horse. *"Do you ride?" — "No, I've never been on a horse."*

1 TRANSITIVE AND INTRANSITIVE to sit on a bicycle or a horse, control it and travel on it

Ⓣ *We passed three men riding motorcycles.*
Ⓘ *I had already ridden for miles that day.*

2 INTRANSITIVE to travel in a vehicle as a passenger □ *He rode in the bus to the hotel.*

ring ✪ [rɪŋ]

rings	3rd person present
ringing	present participle
rang	past tense
rung	past participle

TRANSITIVE AND INTRANSITIVE to make the sound of a bell

Ⓘ *The school bell rang.*
Ⓣ *They had rung the bell but nobody had come to the door.*

PHRASAL VERBS

ring something in

to accompany the arrival of with noise and celebration □ *...a huge party to ring in the new millennium*

ring out or **ring something out**

1 to send forth a loud resounding noise or to resound as a loud noise □ *A second shout rang out.*

2 to accompany the arrival of with noise and celebration □ *Ring out the old year!*

ring up or **ring somthing up**

to record on a cash register □ *I'll ring up your purchases now.* □ *You can ring these items up for me please?*

rip [rɪp]

rips	3rd person present
ripping	present participle
ripped	past tense & past participle

TRANSITIVE AND INTRANSITIVE to tear something quickly, or be torn quickly

Ⓣ *I ripped my shirt when I fell.*
Ⓘ *He heard his jeans rip.*

PHRASAL VERBS

rip someone off

to cheat someone by charging too much for goods or services (informal) □ *People are buying these products and getting ripped off.*

rip something up

to tear something into small pieces □ *He ripped up the letter and threw it in the fire.*

rise ✪ [raiz]

rises	3rd person present
rising	present participle
rose	past tense
risen	past participle

INTRANSITIVE

1 to move upwards □ *We could see black smoke rising from the chimney.*

2 to stand up (formal) □ *He rose slowly from the chair.*

3 to get out of bed (formal) □ *Tony rose early.*

4 When the sun or the moon rises, it appears in the sky. □ *He wanted to be over the top of the hill before the sun had risen.*

5 to increase □ *His income had risen by $5,000.*

roll [roʊl]

rolls	3rd person present
rolling	present participle
rolled	past tense & past participle

1 TRANSITIVE AND INTRANSITIVE to move something along a surface, turning over many times, or to move in this way

T *I rolled a ball to the baby.*

I *The pencil rolled off the desk.*

2 INTRANSITIVE to move quickly down a surface □ *Tears rolled down her cheeks.*

3 rolled into one If something is several things **rolled into one**, it combines the main features or qualities of those things. □ *If I had to compare this movie to anything else I would say it's like Vertigo, Memento, Matrix, Bond, and Heat, all rolled into one.*

PHRASAL VERB

roll something up

to form something into the shape of a ball or a tube □ *Steve rolled up the newspaper into a long tube.*

rub [rʌb]

rubs	3rd person present
rubbing	present participle
rubbed	past tense & past participle

TRANSITIVE

1 to move a cloth or your fingers back and forth over something □ *She took off her glasses and rubbed them with a soft cloth.*

2 to spread a substance over a surface using your hand □ *He rubbed oil into my back.*

PHRASAL VERB

rub something in

to make someone feel even worse about a bad result or event (informal) □ *Thurston's successful conversion put the Broncos back in front and then they rubbed it in by scoring another touchdown.*

rule [ruːl]

rules	3rd person present
ruling	present participle
ruled	past tense & past participle

TRANSITIVE AND INTRANSITIVE to control the affairs of a country

T *He ruled an empire of 50 million people.*

I *King Hussein of Jordan ruled for 46 years.*

PHRASAL VERB

rule something out

to decide or mean that a course of action, an idea, or a solution is impossible or not practical □ *A knee injury ruled the player out of the World Cup.*

run ✪ [rʌn]

runs	3rd person present
running	present participle
ran	past tense
run	past participle

1 INTRANSITIVE to move very quickly on your legs □ *It's very dangerous to run across the road.*

2 INTRANSITIVE to go in a particular direction □ *The road runs east from Hanover to Littlestown.*

3 TRANSITIVE to be in charge of a business or an activity □ *She runs a restaurant in San Francisco.*

4 INTRANSITIVE to be switched on and working □ *Sam waited in the car, with the engine running.*

5 TRANSITIVE AND INTRANSITIVE to start a process and let it continue

T *He ran a lot of tests.*

I *This program runs on a standard personal computer.*

6 INTRANSITIVE to take passengers between two places □ *A bus runs between the mall and the retirement community.*

7 INTRANSITIVE to flow in a particular direction □ *Tears were running down her cheeks.*

PHRASAL VERBS

run away

to leave a place because you are unhappy or afraid there □ *The girl turned and ran away.*

run into someone

to meet someone unexpectedly □ *He ran into William in the supermarket.*

run into someone or something

to hit someone or something with a

vehicle □ *The driver was going too fast and had run into a tree.*

run off

to go away from a place when you should stay there □ *Our dog is always running off.*

run out of something

to have no more of something left □ *We ran out of milk this morning.*

run someone over

to hit someone with a vehicle so that they fall to the ground □ *A police car ran him over.*

run through something

1 to practice a performance or a series of actions □ *Doug listened while I ran through the routine again.*

2 to read or mention all the items on a list quickly □ *I ran through the options with him.*

saw ✪ [sɑː]

saws	3rd person present
sawing	present participle
sawed	past tense
sawn	past participle

TRANSITIVE AND INTRANSITIVE to cut something with a saw

Ⓘ *He has sawn through the bars of his jail cell and escaped.*

Ⓣ *I sawed the dead branches off the tree.*

say ✪ [seɪ]

says	3rd person present
saying	present participle
said	past tense & past participle

> **Say** or **tell**? Use **say** with the actual words that someone speaks, or before **that** with reported speech. *He said "I don't feel well." He said that he didn't feel well.* Remember: You **say something to someone**. *What did she say to you?* You **tell someone something**. *He told Ali the news.* **Tell** is used to report information that is given to someone. *I told Rachel I got the job.* **Tell** can also be used with a 'to' infinitive to report an order or instruction. *My mother told me to eat my dinner.*

TRANSITIVE

1 to speak words □ *I packed and said goodbye to Charlie.*

2 to give information in writing or in numbers □ *The clock said four minutes past eleven.*

3 you can say that again used for showing strong agreement with what someone has just said *(informal)* □ *"Must have been a difficult job." — "You can say that again."*

scoop [skup]

scoops	3rd person present
scooping	present participle
scooped	past tense & past participle

TRANSITIVE to remove something from a container with your hand or with a spoon □ *He was scooping dog food out of a can.*

PHRASAL VERBS

scoop something out

to remove part of something using a spoon or other tool □ *Cut a melon in half and scoop out the seeds.*

scoop something up

to put your hands under something and lift it □ *Use both hands to scoop up the leaves.*

see ✪ [si]

sees	3rd person present
seeing	present participle
saw	past tense
seen	past participle

> **See** or **watch**? You use **see** to talk about things that you notice using your eyes. You often use **can** in this case. *I can see you!* If you want to say that someone is paying attention to something they can see, you say that they **are looking at** it or **watching** it. In general, you **look at** something that is not moving, while you **watch** something that is moving or changing. *I asked him to look at the picture… They watched the children playing.*

TRANSITIVE AND INTRANSITIVE

1 to notice something using your eyes
T *Did you see that policeman?*
I *It's dark and I can't see.*

2 to visit or meet someone □ *I saw him yesterday.*

3 to watch a play, film, or sports event
□ *I saw a great film last night.*

4 to understand something □ *Oh, I see what you're saying.*

5 to find out information or a fact about something □ *Let me see what's on TV next.*

6 to experience a particular event
□ *I have seen many changes here over the past decade.*

7 I'll or we'll see used for saying that you will decide something later □ *"Can we go swimming tomorrow?" — "We'll see. Maybe."*

8 let's see used when you are trying to remember something □ *Let's see. Where did I leave my purse?*

9 see you used for saying goodbye to someone *(informal)* □ *"Talk to you later." — "All right. See you."*

see someone off

to go to a station or airport with someone in order to say goodbye to them
□ *Ben went to the airport to see Jackie off.*

see to someone or something

to deal with someone or something that needs attention □ *Franklin saw to the luggage.*

seek ○ [sik]

seeks	3rd person present
seeking	present participle
sought	past tense & past participle

TRANSITIVE to try to find or get something *(formal)* □ *They are seeking work in hotels and bars.* □ *The couple sought help from a counselor.*

sell ○ [sɛl]

sells	3rd person present
selling	present participle
sold	past tense & past participle

TRANSITIVE

1 to let someone have something that you own in return for money □ *Emily sold the paintings to an art gallery.*

2 to make something available for people to buy □ *This store sells newspapers and candy.*

sell out

to not have any tickets left because they have all been sold □ *Football games often sell out fast.*

sell out of something

to sell all of your supply of something
□ *The supermarket sold out of milk yesterday.*

send ○ [sɛnd]

sends	3rd person present
sending	present participle
sent	past tense & past participle

TRANSITIVE

1 to make a message or a package go to someone □ *Hannah sent me a letter last week.* □ *I sent you an email. Did you get it?*

2 to make someone go somewhere □ *His parents sent him to the supermarket to buy a few things.*

send for someone

to send someone a message asking them to come and see you □ *You might have to send for the doctor.*

send for something

to write and ask for something to be sent to you □ *Send for your free catalog today.*

send something off

to send something somewhere using the mail □ *He sent off copies of his book for people to read.*

set ○ [sɛt]

sets	3rd person present
setting	present participle
set	past tense & past participle

1 TRANSITIVE to put something somewhere carefully □ *She set the vase down gently on the table.*

2 TRANSITIVE to make a clock ready to use □ *I set my alarm clock for seven o'clock every morning.*

3 TRANSITIVE to decide what a date or a price will be □ *They have finally set the date of their wedding.*

4 INTRANSITIVE When the sun sets, it goes down in the sky. □ *They watched the sun set behind the hills.*

5 TRANSITIVE to prepare the table for a meal by putting plates, glasses, knives, forks, and spoons on it □ *Could you set the table for dinner, please?*

6 set fire to something or set something on fire to make something burn □ *Angry protestors threw stones and set cars on fire.* □ *I struck a match and set fire to the papers.*

7 set someone free to cause someone to be free □ *They agreed to set the prisoners free.*

PHRASAL VERBS

set something aside
to keep something available for a particular use or purpose □ *Try to set aside time each day to relax.*

set someone or something back
to cause a delay □ *This mistake has set back our efforts to end the war.*

set off
to start going somewhere □ *Nick set off for his farmhouse in Connecticut.*

set something off
to make an alarm ring or a bomb explode □ *Someone set off a fire alarm.*

set something out
to arrange or display something □ *She set out the cups and saucers.*

set something up
to start or arrange something □ *He plans to set up his own business.*

settle ['sɛtəl]

settles	3rd person present
settling	present participle
settled	past tense & past participle

1 TRANSITIVE to decide what to do about an argument or a problem by talking about it □ *They agreed to try again to settle the dispute.*

2 INTRANSITIVE to start living in a place permanently □ *He visited Paris and eventually settled there.*

3 INTRANSITIVE to sit down and make yourself comfortable □ *Brandon settled in front of the television.*

PHRASAL VERBS

settle down
1 to become calm after being excited □ *Come on, kids. Time to settle down and go to sleep now.*

2 to start living a quiet life in one place, especially after getting married or buying a house □ *One day I'll want to settle down and have a family.*

settle in
to become used to living in a new place, doing a new job, or going to a new school □ *I enjoyed country life once I settled in.*

settle up
to pay a bill or a debt □ *When we asked to settle up, he reduced our bill by 50 percent.*

sew ✪ [sou]

sews	3rd person present
sewing	present participle
sewed	past tense
sewn	past participle

TRANSITIVE AND INTRANSITIVE to join pieces of cloth together using a needle and thread

I *Mrs. Roberts taught her daughter to sew.*

T *She had sewn the dresses on her sewing machine.*

T *She mended socks and sewed clothes at night.*

shake ✪ [ʃeik]

shakes	3rd person present
shaking	present participle
shook	past tense
shaken	past participle

TRANSITIVE AND INTRANSITIVE

1 to move quickly back and forth or up and down

⊡ *My whole body was shaking with fear.*

⊡ *"Did you see Crystal?" Kathryn shook her head.*

2 to hold something and move it quickly up and down ⊡ *Always shake the bottle before you pour out the medicine.* ⊡ *The mixture should always be shaken well before use.*

3 shake hands to say hello or goodbye to someone by holding their right hand in your own right hand and moving it up and down ⊡ *Michael shook hands with Burke.* ⊡ *The two men shook hands.*

4 shake your head to move your head from side to side in order to say "no" ⊡ *He shook his head, but said nothing.*

shall

➡ See *Key Verb* entry on p. 216

shed ✪ [ʃed]

sheds	3rd person present
shedding	present participle
shed	past tense & past participle

TRANSITIVE

1 When a tree sheds its leaves, its leaves fall off, usually in the fall. When an animal sheds hair or skin, some of its hair or skin drops off. ⊡ *The animals regularly shed their hair like cats or dogs.*

2 to get rid of something ⊡ *The company is to shed 700 jobs.*

3 If you shed tears, you cry. ⊡ *They will shed a few tears at their daughter's wedding.*

4 To shed blood means to kill people in a violent way. ⊡ *My family have fought in wars and shed blood for this country.*

shine ✪ [ʃaɪn]

shines	3rd person present
shining	present participle
shone, shined	past tense & past participle

The form **shone** is used as the past tense and past participle. The form **shined** is used as the past tense and past participle for meaning **4**.

1 INTRANSITIVE to give out bright light

⊡ *Today it's warm and the sun is shining.*

2 TRANSITIVE to point a light somewhere

⊡ *The guard shone a light in his face.*

3 INTRANSITIVE to reflect light ⊡ *The sea shone in the silver moonlight.*

4 TRANSITIVE to rub the surface of something in order to make it shine ⊡ *I shined my shoes each day until I could see my face in them.*

shoot ✪ [ʃuːt]

shoots	3rd person present
shooting	present participle
shot	past tense & past participle

1 TRANSITIVE to kill or injure a person or animal by firing a gun at them ⊡ *They shoot several hundred elk a year here.*

2 INTRANSITIVE to fire a bullet from a weapon such as a gun ⊡ *They started shooting at us.*

3 INTRANSITIVE to move in a particular direction quickly and suddenly ⊡ *A van shot out of the parking lot and crashed into the back of their car.*

4 TRANSITIVE to make a film or take photographs using a camera ⊡ *He wants to shoot his film in Cuba.*

5 INTRANSITIVE to try to score by kicking, throwing, or hitting the ball toward the goal in sports such as football or basketball ⊡ *He tried to shoot at the basket.*

PHRASAL VERBS

shoot something down

to reject something as unacceptable

⊡ *Once Courtney got wind of the suggestion she immediately shot it down as "stupid."*

shoot up

to grow or increase very quickly ⊡ *Sales have shot up by 9%.*

should

➡ See *Key Verb* entry on p. 220

show ✪ [ʃoʊ]

shows	3rd person present
showing	present participle

shall [ʃəl, strong ʃæl] and will [wɪl]

MODAL VERBS

You use the modal verb **will**, followed by the base form of a main verb, to express simple future time in English. The modal verb **shall** is often used in suggestions, or offers of help, and in various kinds of official language.

> *Shall I cook supper?*
> *Shall we go to the movies tonight?*
> *No additive shall be deemed safe if it induces cancer when ingested by man or animal.*

Contracted forms

The contracted form of both **shall** and **will** is **'ll**. This means that it is impossible to tell the difference between the two forms in spoken English.

> *He'll be home soon.*
> *We'll have to hurry or we'll be late.*

The contracted negative form of **will** is **won't**. The contracted negative form of **shall** is **shan't**. This form is rare, and is used mainly in British English.

> *Eve won't speak to Harriet.*
> *I shan't say a word.*

Main senses

1 **Shall** is used with *I* and *we* in offers, suggestions and requests for advice, presented in the form of questions.

Shall I get the keys?
Let's play one more hand, shall we?
What shall I do?

2 **Shall** is used by governments and courts in writing laws, rules, and decisions to indicate that they have the authority of enforcement, or that people must comply or obey.

No structure shall be erected less than twenty feet from a property boundary.
The Central People's Government shall be responsible for the foreign affairs of the Hong Kong Special Administrative Region.

3 **Shall** or **will** is used with **I** and **we** to show intentions, to make promises, and to refer to things that you are sure will happen to you in the future. **Shall** is considered formal in American English and is not used as frequently as **will**.

We shall/will be in touch.
I shall/will miss him terribly.
I shall/will know more tomorrow, I hope.

4 **Will** is used with **you**, **he**, **she**, **it** and **they**, to reassure someone about something.

He will be well treated.
You will have your money next week.

5 **Will** is used for insisting on something.

You will do exactly what I tell you!

6 **Will** is used for making polite requests and for giving invitations.

Will you help me look for my purse?
Will you come to lunch on Friday?

7 **Will** is used for giving orders.

> *You will finish your homework before you watch TV.*
> *Luella, will you please be quiet!*

8 **Will** is used for predicting.

> *They'll no doubt be late as usual.*
> *I think it will probably rain tomorrow.*

9 **Will** is used for saying that someone is willing to do something. You use **will not** or **won't** to say that someone refuses to do something.

> *All right; I'll forgive you.*
> *I won't let you pay for a taxi. I'll drive you to the airport myself.*

showed past tense
shown past participle

1 TRANSITIVE to prove that a situation exists □ *Research shows that certain foods can help prevent headaches.*

2 TRANSITIVE to let someone see something □ *She showed me her engagement ring.*

3 TRANSITIVE to teach someone how to do something □ *Claire showed us how to make pasta.*

4 INTRANSITIVE to be easy to notice □ *When I feel angry, it shows.*

PHRASAL VERBS

show off
to try to make people admire you □ *He spent the entire evening showing off.*

show someone around
to go around a place with someone, pointing out its interesting features □ *She showed him around the farm.*

show something off
to show something to a lot of people because you are proud of it □ *Naomi was showing off her engagement ring.*

show up
to arrive at the place where you agreed to meet someone □ *By five, he still hadn't shown up.*

shrink ✪ [ʃrɪŋk]

shrinks 3rd person present
shrinking present participle
shrank past tense
shrunk past participle

INTRANSITIVE to become smaller in size □ *Dad's slacks shrank after just one wash.* □ *All my sweaters have shrunk.*

shut ✪ [ʃʌt]

shuts 3rd person present
shutting present participle
shut past tense & past participle

TRANSITIVE AND INTRANSITIVE to close
Ⓣ *Please shut the gate.*
Ⓘ *The screen door shut gently.*

PHRASAL VERB

shut up
used for telling someone, in a rude way, to stop talking □ *Just shut up, will you?*

sign [saɪn]

signs 3rd person present
signing present participle
signed past tense & past participle

TRANSITIVE

1 to put your signature on a document □ *World leaders have signed an agreement to protect the environment.*

2 to arrange for someone to sign a contract agreeing to work for an organization for a period of time □ *They've just signed a new short-stop.*

PHRASAL VERBS

sign for something
to officially state that you have received something, by signing a form or book □ *When the mailman delivers your order, you'll have to sign for it.*

sign in
to officially show that you have arrived at a place by signing a book or form □ *I signed in and went straight to my room.*

sign out
to officially show that you have left a place by signing a book or form □ *Workers must sign out when they leave the office.*

sign up for something
to officially agree to work for an organization or do a course of study by signing a contract or form □ *He signed up for a driving course.*

sing ✪ [sɪŋ]

sings 3rd person present
singing present participle
sang past tense
sung past participle

TRANSITIVE AND INTRANSITIVE to make music with your voice
Ⓘ *I love singing.*
Ⓣ *My brother and I used to sing this song.*
Ⓣ *...an aria sung by Luciano Pavarotti.*

should [ʃəd, strong ʃʊd]

MODAL VERB

You use **should** for expressing obligation in the present or future, for talking about regrets about the past, and to give advice and instructions. It is also used in some conditional clauses. When you are changing sentences from direct to reported speech, **should** does not change.

Contracted forms

The contracted negative form of **should** is **shouldn't**.

> *You shouldn't tell lies.*

Main senses

1 **Should** is used for saying what would be the right thing to do. Compare ***ought to*** (see pp.203–204).

> *They should do what you suggest.*
> *I should get more exercise.*

2 **Should** is used for giving or asking for advice or instructions.

> *You should always wash your hands before eating.*
> *Should we tell her about it?*

3 **Should** is used for talking about things that are not the case but that you think ought to be.

> *Everyone should live together in peace.*
> *I am not as brave as I should be.*

4 **Should** is used for giving someone an order to do something.

> *All visitors should report to the duty officer.*

5 You use **should** for saying that something is probably true or will probably happen in the way that you describe.

> *The doctor said I should be fine by next week.*
> *You should have no problem passing the exam.*

6 **Should** is used for suggesting that something follows logically from what has just been said.

> *They left here at 6 o'clock, so they should be home by now.*
> *You've studied really hard, so you should pass the exam easily.*

7 **Should** is used for expressing regret about something in the past. Here, **should have** is used, followed by the past participle of the main verb.

> *You should have told me you were ill.*
> *I should have put on sunscreen.*

sing along

to sing while you are listening to someone else perform a piece of music □ *Fifteen hundred people all sang along.*

sink ✪ [sɪŋk]

sinks	3rd person present
sinking	present participle
sank	past tense
sunk	past participle

INTRANSITIVE

1 to go below the surface of the water □ *The boat had hit the rocks and sunk.*

2 to move slowly down, to a lower level □ *The sun was sinking in the west.*

sink in

to be fully understood □ *The news sank in slowly.*

sit ✪ [sɪt]

sits	3rd person present
sitting	present participle
sat	past tense & past participle

INTRANSITIVE

1 to have the lower part of your body resting on a chair and the upper part straight □ *Mother was sitting in her chair in the kitchen.*

2 to move your body down until you are sitting on something □ *He set the cases against a wall and sat on them.*

sit around

to spend time doing nothing useful (informal) □ *Eve isn't the type to sit around doing nothing.*

sit back

to relax and not become involved in something that is happening □ *Get everyone talking and then sit back and enjoy the show.*

sit down

to move your body down until you are sitting □ *Mom sat down beside me.*

sit through something

to stay until something has finished, although you are not enjoying it □ *He sat through the play with an angry expression.*

sit up

1 to change the position of your body, so that you are sitting instead of lying down □ *She felt dizzy when she sat up.*

2 to not go to bed although it is very late □ *We sat up, drinking coffee and talking.*

sleep ✪ [slip]

sleeps	3rd person present
sleeping	present participle
slept	past tense & past participle

INTRANSITIVE to rest with your eyes closed and with no activity in your mind or body □ *I slept badly last night — it was too hot.*

sleep through something

to continue to sleep when something happens or when there is a lot of noise □ *They slept right through the alarm.*

slide ✪ [slaid]

slides	3rd person present
sliding	present participle
slid	past tense & past participle

TRANSITIVE AND INTRANSITIVE to move quickly and smoothly over a surface

Ⓣ *She slid the door open.*

Ⓘ *She slid across the ice on her stomach.*

sling ✪ [slɪŋ]

slings	3rd person present
slinging	present participle
slung	past tense & past participle

TRANSITIVE to throw something in a rough way □ *She slung the sack over her shoulder.*

slip [slɪp]

slips	3rd person present
slipping	present participle
slipped	past tense & past participle

1 INTRANSITIVE to accidentally slide and fall □ *He slipped on the wet grass.*

2 INTRANSITIVE to slide out of position □ *Grandpa's glasses slipped down his nose.*

3 INTRANSITIVE to go somewhere quickly and quietly □ *In the morning she quietly slipped out of the house.*

4 TRANSITIVE to put something somewhere quickly and quietly □ *I slipped the letter into my pocket.*

PHRASAL VERB

slip up

to make a mistake □ *We slipped up a few times, but no one noticed.*

slit ✪ [slɪt]

slits	3rd person present
slitting	present participle
slit	past tense & past participle

TRANSITIVE to make a long narrow cut in something □ *He slit the envelope open.*

slow [sloʊ]

slows	3rd person present
slowing	present participle
slowed	past tense & past participle

TRANSITIVE AND INTRANSITIVE to start to move or happen more slowly, or to cause this to happen

Ⓣ *The treatment slows the progress of the disease.*

Ⓘ *The economy has slowed in recent months.*

PHRASAL VERB

slow down or slow something down

to start to move or happen more slowly, or to cause this to happen □ *The bus slowed down for the next stop.* □ *Use your gears to slow the car down.*

smash [smæʃ]

smashes	3rd person present
smashing	present participle
smashed	past tense & past participle

TRANSITIVE AND INTRANSITIVE

1 to break into many pieces or to cause this to happen

Ⓣ *Someone smashed a bottle.*

Ⓘ *Two glasses fell and smashed into pieces.*

2 to get through something by hitting and breaking it

Ⓣ *Soldiers smashed their way into his office.*

Ⓘ *The trucks smashed through the gates.*

3 to move something with great force against something else □ *He smashed his fist into Anthony's face.*

PHRASAL VERB

smash something up

to completely destroy something by hitting it and breaking it into many pieces □ *The gang smashed up furniture and broke windows.*

soak [soʊk]

soaks	3rd person present
soaking	present participle
soaked	past tense & past participle

1 TRANSITIVE AND INTRANSITIVE to put something into a liquid and leave it there, or to be left in a liquid

Ⓣ *Soak the beans for 2 hours.*

Ⓘ *He left the dishes to soak.*

2 TRANSITIVE to make something very wet □ *The water soaked his jacket.*

3 INTRANSITIVE to pass through something □ *Blood soaked through the bandages.*

PHRASAL VERB

soak something up

to take in a liquid □ *Use a towel to soak up the water.*

sort [sɔrt]

sorts	3rd person present
sorting	present participle
sorted	past tense & past participle

TRANSITIVE to separate things into different groups □ *He sorted the documents into their folders.*

PHRASAL VERB

sort something out

1 to separate things into different groups □ *I was just sorting out some old clothes.*

2 to deal with a problem successfully

☐ The two countries have sorted out their disagreement.

SOW ✪ [sou]

sows	3rd person present
sowing	present participle
sowed	past tense
sown	past participle

TRANSITIVE to plant seeds in the ground ☐ Sow the seeds in a warm place in early March. ☐ The seeds that I sowed did quite well. ☐ As of June 27, 97% of the soy crop was sown, the USDA said earlier this week.

speak ✪ [spik]

speaks	3rd person present
speaking	present participle
spoke	past tense
spoken	past participle

> See note at **talk**.

1 INTRANSITIVE to use your voice in order to say something ☐ It was the first time either of us had spoken.

2 INTRANSITIVE to make a speech ☐ He spoke at the Democratic Convention.

3 TRANSITIVE to know a foreign language and be able to have a conversation in it ☐ He speaks English.

PHRASAL VERB

speak up

to speak more loudly ☐ I'm quite deaf — you'll have to speak up.

speed ✪ [spid]

speeds	3rd person present
speeding	present participle
sped, speeded	past tense & past participle

> Use **sped** in meaning **1** and **speeded** in meaning **2** and for the phrasal verb.

INTRANSITIVE

1 to move or travel somewhere quickly, usually in a vehicle ☐ The train sped through the tunnel at 186 mph.

2 to drive a vehicle faster than the legal speed limit ☐ Police stopped him because he was speeding.

PHRASAL VERBS

speed something up

to make something happen more quickly than before ☐ We need to speed up a solution to the problem.

speed up

to start to happen more quickly ☐ My breathing speeded up a bit.

spend ✪ [spɛnd]

spends	3rd person present
spending	present participle
spent	past tense & past participle

> See note at **pass**.

TRANSITIVE

1 to pay money for things that you want or need ☐ I have spent all my money.

2 to use your time doing something ☐ She spends hours working on her garden.

spin ✪ [spɪn]

spins	3rd person present
spinning	present participle
spun	past tense & past participle

TRANSITIVE AND INTRANSITIVE

1 to turn quickly around a central point, or to make something turn in this way

Ⅰ The disc spins 3,600 times a minute.

Ⅰ He spun the steering wheel and turned the car around.

2 to make thread by twisting together pieces of wool or cotton ☐ It's a machine for spinning wool.

spit ✪ [spɪt]

spits	3rd person present
spitting	present participle
spat, spit	past tense & past participle

TRANSITIVE AND INTRANSITIVE to force a small amount of liquid or food out of your mouth

Ⅰ Don't spit your gum on the ground!

Ⅰ They spat at me and laughed at me.

PHRASAL VERB

spit up or **spit something up**

(informal)

to return food from your stomach to your mouth; vomit □ *Annie spit up all over the kitchen table when she saw what they were doing in the hammock.* □ *After the second round of compressions the little boy spat up about half a cup of water.*

split ✪ [splɪt]

splits	3rd person present
splitting	present participle
split	past tense & past participle

1 INTRANSITIVE to break into two or more parts □ *The ship split in two during a storm.*

2 TRANSITIVE to divide something into two or more parts □ *Split the chicken in half.*

3 TRANSITIVE AND INTRANSITIVE to break, producing a long crack or tear, or to cause something to break in this way
Ⓘ *My jeans split while I was climbing over the wall.*
Ⓣ *I split my pants.*

4 TRANSITIVE to share something between two or more people □ *Let's split the bill.*

PHRASAL VERB

split up

to stop being in a marriage or romantic relationship together □ *His parents split up when he was ten.*

spread ✪ [spred]

spreads	3rd person present
spreading	present participle
spread	past tense & past participle

1 TRANSITIVE to open something out over a surface □ *She spread a towel on the sand and lay on it.*

2 TRANSITIVE to stretch out parts of your body until they are far apart □ *Sit on the floor, and spread your arms and legs.*

3 TRANSITIVE to put a substance all over a surface □ *She was spreading butter on the bread.*

4 INTRANSITIVE to gradually reach a larger area □ *Information technology has spread across the world.*

PHRASAL VERBS

spread out

to move apart □ *His men moved, spreading out into two teams.*

spread something out

to arrange something over a surface, so that all of it can be seen or used easily □ *Tom spread out a map of Scandinavia.*

spring ✪ [sprɪŋ]

springs	3rd person present
springing	present participle
sprang	past tense
sprung	past participle

INTRANSITIVE to jump suddenly or quickly □ *The lion roared once and sprang.* □ *They had both sprung to their feet and were looking down at me.*

stand ✪ [stænd]

stands	3rd person present
standing	present participle
stood	past tense & past participle

INTRANSITIVE

1 to be on your feet □ *She was standing beside my bed.*

2 to move so that you are on your feet □ *Becker stood and shook hands with Ben.*

3 to be in a place □ *The house stands alone on top of a hill.*

4 can't stand someone or something used for saying that you dislike someone or something very strongly (*informal*) □ *I can't stand that awful man.* □ *I can't stand that smell.*

5 stand aside/stand back to move a short distance away □ *I stood aside to let her pass me.*

PHRASAL VERBS

stand aside

to move a short distance away □ *I stood aside to let her pass me.*

stand by

1 to be ready to help □ *Police officers are standing by in case of trouble.*

2 to not do anything to stop something

bad from happening □ *Would you stand by and watch people suffering?*

stand for something

to be a short form of a word □ *U.S. stands for United States.*

stand in for someone

to take someone's place or do their job, because they are ill or away □ *He will stand in for Mr. Goh when he is on vacation.*

stand out

to be very easy to see □ *The black necklace stood out against her white dress.*

stand up

to move so that you are on your feet □ *When I walked in, they all stood up.*

stand up for someone or something

to support a person or a belief □ *Nelson Mandela stood up for his people and his beliefs.*

stand up to someone

to defend yourself against someone who is more powerful than you □ *He was too afraid to stand up to her.*

start [start]

starts	3rd person present
starting	present participle
started	past tense & past participle

1 TRANSITIVE to do something that you were not doing before □ *Susanna started working in TV in 2005.*

2 INTRANSITIVE to take place from a particular time □ *The fire started in an upstairs room.*

3 TRANSITIVE to create something or cause it to begin □ *She has started a child care center in Lancaster.*

4 TRANSITIVE AND INTRANSITIVE If a car or a machine starts, or if you start it, it begins to work.

Ⓣ *He started the car and drove off.*

Ⓘ *The engine won't start.*

5 to start with used for introducing the first of a number of things □ *To start with, you need her name and address.*

PHRASAL VERBS

start off

to do something as the first part of an activity □ *She started off by clearing some space on the table.*

start over

to begin something again from the beginning □ *I did it all wrong and had to start over.*

stay [stei]

stays	3rd person present
staying	present participle
stayed	past tense & past participle

1 INTRANSITIVE to continue to be where you are, and not to leave □ *"Stay here," Trish said. "I'll bring the car to you."*

2 INTRANSITIVE to live somewhere for a short time □ *Gordon stayed at The Park Hotel, Milan.* □ *Can't you stay for a few more days?*

3 LINKING VERB to continue to be in a particular state or situation □ *Exercise is one of the best ways to stay healthy.*

PHRASAL VERBS

stay away

to not go to a place □ *Most workers stayed away from work during the strike.*

stay in

to remain at home and not go out □ *We decided to stay in and have dinner at home.*

stay on

to remain somewhere after other people have left or after the time when you were going to leave □ *He arranged to stay on in Adelaide.*

stay out

to remain away from home at night □ *I met some friends and stayed out until eleven or twelve.*

stay up

not to go to bed at your usual time □ *I used to stay up late with my mom and watch movies.*

steal ✪ [stil]

steals	3rd person present
stealing	present participle
stole	past tense
stolen	past participle

TRANSITIVE AND INTRANSITIVE to take something from someone without their permission

☐ *It's wrong to steal.*

☐ *They said he stole a small boy's bicycle.*

☐ *Someone had stolen the key for the lock.*

stick ✪ [stɪk]

sticks	3rd person present
sticking	present participle
stuck	past tense & past participle

1 TRANSITIVE to join one thing to another using a sticky substance

☐ *Now stick your picture on a piece of paper.*

2 TRANSITIVE to push a pointed object into something ☐ *The doctor stuck the needle into Joe's arm.*

3 TRANSITIVE to put something somewhere *(informal)* ☐ *He folded the papers and stuck them in his desk.*

4 INTRANSITIVE to become joined to something and be difficult to remove

☐ *The paper sometimes sticks to the bottom of the cake.*

PHRASAL VERBS

stick around

to stay where you are *(informal)* ☐ *I didn't stick around long enough to find out.*

stick by someone

to continue to give someone support ☐ *All my friends stuck by me during the difficult times.*

stick out

to continue further than the main part of something ☐ *His two front teeth stick out slightly.*

stick something out

to push something forward or away from you ☐ *He stuck his hand out and he said, "Good evening."*

stick to something

to not change your mind about a promise or a decision ☐ *We are waiting to see if he sticks to his promise.*

stick up

to point upwards ☐ *His hair stuck up.*

stick up for someone or **something**

to support someone or something, and say that they are right ☐ *My father always sticks up for me.*

sting ✪ [stɪŋ]

stings	3rd person present
stinging	present participle
stung	past tense & past participle

1 TRANSITIVE AND INTRANSITIVE If a plant, an animal or an insect stings you, a pointed part of it is pushed into your skin so that you feel a sharp pain.

☐ *She was stung by a bee.*

☐ *This type of bee rarely stings.*

2 INTRANSITIVE If a part of your body stings, you feel a sharp pain there. ☐ *His cheeks were stinging from the cold wind.*

stink ✪ [stɪŋk]

stinks	3rd person present
stinking	present participle
stank	past tense
stunk	past participle

INTRANSITIVE to smell very bad ☐ *The place stinks of fried onions.* ☐ *We all stank and nobody cared.* ☐ *The canals have always stunk in the summer.*

stretch [stretʃ]

stretches	3rd person present
stretching	present participle
stretched	past tense & past participle

1 INTRANSITIVE to cover all of a particular distance ☐ *The line of cars stretched for several miles.*

2 TRANSITIVE AND INTRANSITIVE to put your arms or legs out very straight

☐ *Try stretching your legs and pulling your toes upward.*

☐ *He yawned and stretched.*

3 INTRANSITIVE to become longer and thinner ☐ *Can you feel your leg muscles stretching?*

stretch out

to lie with your legs and body in a straight line □ *The bathtub was too small to stretch out in.*

stretch something out

to hold out a part of your body straight □ *He stretched out his hand to touch me.*

stride ✪ [straid]

strides	3rd person present
striding	present participle
strode	past tense & past participle

INTRANSITIVE to walk with long steps □ *The farmer strode across the field.*

strike ✪ [straik]

strikes	3rd person present
striking	present participle
struck	past tense & past participle
stricken	past participle

1 TRANSITIVE to hit someone or something *(formal)* □ *She took two steps forward and struck him across the face.*

2 INTRANSITIVE to have a quick and violent effect □ *A storm struck in the northeastern United States on Saturday.*

3 TRANSITIVE to come suddenly into your mind □ *A thought struck her. Was she jealous of her mother?*

4 TRANSITIVE AND INTRANSITIVE When a clock strikes, it makes a sound so that people know what the time is.

Ⓣ *The clock struck nine.*

Ⓘ *Finally, the clock strikes.*

5 INTRANSITIVE to refuse to work, usually in order to try to get more money □ *Workers have the right to strike.*

6 strike a match to make a match produce a flame by moving it against something rough □ *Duncan struck a match and lit the fire.*

strip [strip]

strips	3rd person present
stripping	present participle
stripped	past tense & past participle

1 INTRANSITIVE to remove the clothes from your body □ *We all stripped and jumped into the lake.*

2 TRANSITIVE to remove everything that covers something □ *I stripped the beds.*

strip off or strip off something

to take off your clothes □ *I stripped off and got into the bath.* □ *He stripped off his wet clothes and stepped into the shower.*

stub [stʌb]

stubs	3rd person present
stubbing	present participle
stubbed	past tense & past participle

TRANSITIVE to hurt your toe by accidentally kicking something □ *I stubbed my toe against a table leg.*

stub something out

to stop a cigarette from burning by pressing it against something hard □ *We ask all visitors to stub out their cigarettes.*

sum [sʌm]

sums	3rd person present
summing	present participle
summed	past tense & past participle

sum something up

to say or do something that shows what someone or something is like □ *Google summed up the current version of Image Search by saying that it is a simple interface with powerful tools.*

sum up

to briefly describe the main features of something □ *Well, to sum up, what are you trying to say?*

swear ✪ [sweᵊr]

swears	3rd person present
swearing	present participle
swore	past tense
sworn	past participle

1 INTRANSITIVE to use language that is considered to be offensive □ *It's wrong to swear and shout.* □ *They swore at them and ran off.*

2 TRANSITIVE to promise in a serious way that you will do something □ *I swear to do everything I can to help you.* □ *We have sworn to fight cruelty wherever we find it.*

sweep ● [swiːp]

sweeps	3rd person present
sweeping	present participle
swept	past tense & past participle

TRANSITIVE

1 to push dirt off an area using a brush with a long handle □ *The owner of the shop was sweeping his floor.*

2 to push objects off something with a quick smooth movement of your arm □ *She swept the cards from the table.*

PHRASAL VERB

sweep someone up in something

to involve someone in a situation in which they have no control □ *Native American children swept up in the Iowa child welfare system face many perils.*

swell ● [swel]

swells	3rd person present
swelling	present participle
swelled	past tense & past participle
swollen	past participle

INTRANSITIVE to become larger and thicker than normal □ *Do your legs swell at night?* □ *His eye swelled up.* □ *...his swollen knee.*

swim ● [swim]

swims	3rd person present
swimming	present participle
swam	past tense
swum	past participle

TRANSITIVE AND INTRANSITIVE to move through water by making movements with your arms and legs

Ⓘ *She learned to swim when she was 10.*
Ⓣ *I always swam a mile a day.*

Ⓘ *The man on the beach had swum in from a boat.*

swing ● [swiŋ]

swings	3rd person present
swinging	present participle
swung	past tense & past participle

TRANSITIVE AND INTRANSITIVE to move repeatedly back and forth or from side to side through the air, or to cause something to do this

Ⓣ *She swung a bottle of soda in her hand.*
Ⓘ *Amber walked beside him, her arms swinging.*

switch [swɪtʃ]

switches	3rd person present
switching	present participle
switched	past tense & past participle

1 INTRANSITIVE to change to something different □ *Companies are switching to cleaner fuels.*

2 TRANSITIVE to replace one thing with another thing □ *They switched the keys, so Karen had the key to my room and I had the key to hers.*

PHRASAL VERBS

switch something off

to stop electrical equipment from working by operating a switch □ *She switched off the coffee machine.*

switch something on

to make electrical equipment start working by operating a switch □ *He switched on the lamp.*

take ● [teik]

takes	3rd person present
taking	present participle
took	past tense
taken	past participle

See note at **bring**.

TRANSITIVE

1 to reach out and get something □ *Let me take your coat.*

2 to carry something with you □ *Don't*

forget to take a map with you.

3 to transport someone somewhere □ *Michael had taken me to the airport.*

4 to steal something □ *They took my wallet.*

5 to need an amount of time □ *The sauce takes 25 minutes to prepare.*

6 to accept something that someone offers you □ *I think you should take my advice.*

7 to choose to travel along a road □ *Take I–83 north to Harrisburg.*

8 to use a vehicle to go from one place to another □ *She took the train to New York.*

9 used for saying that someone does something □ *She was too tired to take a bath.*

10 to study a subject in school □ *Students can take European history and American history.*

11 to do an examination □ *She took her driving test yesterday and passed.*

12 to swallow medicine □ *I try not to take pills of any kind.*

13 **take time off** to not go to work for a time □ *My husband was ill and I had to take time off work to take care of him.*

PHRASAL VERBS

take after someone

to look or behave like an older member of your family □ *Your mom was a smart, brave woman. You take after her.*

take something apart

to separate something into its different parts □ *He took the clock apart and found what was wrong.*

take something away

to remove something □ *The waitress took away the dirty dishes.*

take something back

to return something □ *If you don't like it, I'll take it back to the store.*

take something down

1 to separate a structure into pieces and remove it □ *They took down the wall between the living room and the kitchen.*

2 to write information down □ *I took down his comments in my notebook.*

take something in

to pay attention to something and understand it when you hear or read it □ *Robert took it all in without needing a second explanation.*

take off

When an airplane takes off, it leaves the ground and starts flying. □ *We took off at 11 o'clock.*

take something off

to remove clothes □ *Come in and take off your coat.*

take someone out

to take someone somewhere enjoyable □ *Sophia had taken me out to lunch that day.*

take over or **take something over**

to get control of something □ *I'm going to take over this company one day.* □ *You should stop and have some lunch. I'll take over.*

take something up

to start doing an activity □ *Peter took up tennis at the age of eight.*

take up something

to use an amount of time or space □ *I don't want to take up too much of your time.*

talk [tak]

talks	3rd person present
talking	present participle
talked	past tense & past participle

> **Talk** or **speak**? When you **speak**, you say things: *Did someone speak?* **Talk** is used for describing a conversation or discussion: *I talked about it with my family at dinner.* **Talk** can also be used to describe the activity of saying things, rather than the words that are spoken. *She thought I talked too much.*

INTRANSITIVE

1 to say things to someone □ *They were talking about American food.*

2 to make an informal speech about something □ *He talks to young people*

about the dangers of alcohol.
3 to have formal discussions □ *The two sides still aren't prepared to talk to each other.*

talk someone into something

to persuade someone to do something □ *He talked me into marrying him.*

talk someone out of something

to persuade someone not to do something □ *People tried to talk him out of it, but he insisted.*

talk something over

to discuss something thoroughly and honestly □ *He always talked things over with his friends.*

talk something through

to discuss something thoroughly □ *That's how we cope, by talking things through.*

teach ✪ [titʃ]

teaches	3rd person present
teaching	present participle
taught	past tense & past participle

TRANSITIVE

1 to give someone instructions so that they know about something or know how to do it □ *She taught me to read.*
2 to give lessons in a subject at a school or a college
Ⓣ *Christine teaches biology at Piper High School.*
Ⓘ *Mrs. Green has been teaching part-time for 16 years.*

team [tim]

teams	3rd person present
teaming	present participle
teamed	past tense & past participle

team up or team up with someone

to join someone in order to work together for a particular purpose □ *Police in Maryland and Virginia are teaming up to enforce HOV rules across the region .* □ *Elton teamed up with Eric Clapton to make the record.*

tear ✪ [tɛər]

tears	3rd person present
tearing	present participle
tore	past tense
torn	past participle

TRANSITIVE to pull something into pieces or make a hole in it □ *I tore my coat on a nail.*

tear something up

to tear something such as a piece of paper into small pieces □ *He had torn up the letter and thrown it in the fire.*

tell ✪ [tɛl]

tells	3rd person present
telling	present participle
told	past tense & past participle

> See note at **say**.

TRANSITIVE

1 to give someone information □ *I told Rachel I got the job.*
2 to order someone to do something □ *The police officer told him to get out of his car.*
3 to be able to judge correctly what is happening or what is true □ *I could tell that Tom was tired and bored.*

tell someone apart

to be able to recognize the differences between people and identify them individually □ *The twins are so similar that we cannot tell them apart.*

tell someone off

to speak to someone in an angry or serious way because they have done something wrong □ *He never listened to us when we told him off.*

think ✪ [θɪŋk]

thinks	3rd person present
thinking	present participle
thought	past tense & past participle

1 TRANSITIVE AND INTRANSITIVE to believe something or have an opinion about it

T *I think that it will snow tomorrow.*

I *What do you think of my idea?*

2 INTRANSITIVE to use your mind to consider something □ *She closed her eyes for a moment, trying to think.*

3 think of or about doing something to consider doing something □ *I'm thinking of going to college next year.*

4 think of something used for saying that something comes into your mind □ *I know who he is but I can't think of his name.*

PHRASAL VERBS

think something over

to consider something carefully before you make a decision about it □ *They've offered her the job but she needs to think it over.*

think something up

to invent an idea or plan □ *Julian has thought up a new way of raising money.*

throw ✪ [θrou]

throws	3rd person present
throwing	present participle
threw	past tense
thrown	past participle

TRANSITIVE to move your hand or arm quickly and let go of an object that you are holding, so that it moves through the air □ *The crowd began throwing stones at the police.*

PHRASAL VERBS

throw something away

to get rid of something that you do not want □ *I am glad you didn't throw away that picture, it's beautiful!*

throw someone out

to force someone to leave □ *I was so angry at him that I threw him out of the house.*

throw something out

to get rid of something that you do not want □ *I've decided to throw out all the clothes I never wear.*

throw up

to vomit *(informal)* □ *She said she had thrown up after eating at the restaurant.*

thrust ✪ [θrʌst]

thrusts	3rd person present
thrusting	present participle
thrust	past tense & past participle

TRANSITIVE to push or move something or someone somewhere quickly and with a lot of force □ *They thrust him into the back of a car.*

tip [tɪp]

tips	3rd person present
tipping	present participle
tipped	past tense & past participle

1 INTRANSITIVE to move so that one end is higher than the other □ *The stroller can tip backwards if you hang bags on the handles.*

2 TRANSITIVE to pour something somewhere □ *I picked up the bowl of cereal and tipped it over his head.*

3 TRANSITIVE to give someone some money to thank them for a job they have done for you □ *At the end of the meal, he tipped the waiter.*

PHRASAL VERB

tip something over

to make something fall over □ *He tipped the table over.*

top [tɑp]

tops	3rd person present
topping	present participle
topped	past tense & past participle

PHRASAL VERB

top something up

to fill a container again when it has been partly emptied □ *He topped her glass up.*

track [træk]

tracks	3rd person present
tracking	present participle
tracked	past tense & past participle

TRANSITIVE to try to find animals or people by following the signs or marks that they leave behind □ *We all got up early to track deer in the woods.*

track someone or something down

to find someone or something after a difficult or long search □ *She spent years trying to track down her parents.*

try [traɪ]

tries	3rd person present
trying	present participle
tried	past tense & past participle

TRANSITIVE AND INTRANSITIVE

1 to make an effort to do something
Ⓣ *He tried to help her at work.*
Ⓘ *She doesn't seem to try hard enough.*

2 to use or do something new or different in order to discover what it is like □ *You could try a little cheese melted on the top.*

3 to go to a particular place or person because you think that they may be able to give you what you need □ *Have you tried the local library?*

4 to decide in a law court if someone is guilty of a crime □ *They were arrested and tried for murder.*

try something on

to put on a piece of clothing in order to see if it fits you or if it looks nice □ *Try on the shoes to make sure they fit.*

try something out

to test something in order to find out how useful or effective it is □ *I want to try the boat out next weekend.*

try out for something

to take part in a test to see if you are selected for a team, part, etc. □ *I tried out for the Woodland girls' volleyball team last summer.*

tune [tun]

tunes	3rd person present
tuning	present participle
tuned	past tense & past participle

TRANSITIVE to make small changes to a musical instrument so that it produces the right notes □ *We tune our guitars before we go on stage.*

tune something in

to set a radio or television to a particular station or broadcast □ *Almost 27 million viewers tuned in, a 35% increase over last year's awards ceremony.*

turn [tɜrn]

turns	3rd person present
turning	present participle
turned	past tense & past participle

1 TRANSITIVE AND INTRANSITIVE to move in a different direction, or to make something move in this way
Ⓘ *He turned and walked away.*
Ⓣ *He turned his head left and right.*

2 TRANSITIVE AND INTRANSITIVE to move around in a circle, or to make something move in this way
Ⓘ *The wheels turned very slowly.*
Ⓣ *Turn the key to the right.*

3 TRANSITIVE to move a page in a book so that you can look at the next page
□ *He turned the pages of his photo album.*

4 INTRANSITIVE to find a particular page in a book □ *Please turn to page 236.*

5 LINKING VERB to become □ *The sky turned pale pink.*

6 TRANSITIVE to reach a particular age
□ *He made a million dollars before he turned thirty.*

turn against someone

to stop supporting, trusting, or liking someone □ *Even his former friends turned against him.*

turn around

to move to face the opposite direction □ *I felt a tap on my shoulder and I turned around.*

turn back

to change direction and go toward where you started from □ *The fog got worse, and we decided to turn back.*

turn into something

to become something different □ *In the story, the prince turns into a frog.*

turn out

1 to happen □ *I didn't know my life was going to turn out like this.*

2 to be discovered to be something □ *The smell turned out to be melting plastic light covers.*

turn over

to move so that the top part is on the bottom □ *The car turned over and landed in a river.*

turn someone away

to refuse to allow someone to enter a place □ *The stadium was full, and they were turning people away.*

turn something around

to move something so that it faces the opposite direction □ *I turned the car around and went south.*

turn something down

1 to refuse an offer □ *The company offered me a new contract, but I turned it down.*

2 to make a piece of equipment produce less sound or heat □ *Please turn the TV down!*

turn something off

to make a piece of equipment stop working □ *The light's a bit bright. Can you turn it off?*

turn something on

to make a piece of equipment start working □ *I turned on the television.*

turn something out

to switch off a light □ *Remember to turn the lights out when you leave the building.*

turn something over

to move something so that the top part is on the bottom □ *Liz picked up the envelope and turned it over.*

turn something up

to make a piece of equipment produce more sound or heat □ *I turned the volume up.*

turn to someone

to ask someone for their help □ *She turned to him for support when she lost her job.*

turn up

to arrive □ *They finally turned up at nearly midnight.*

use [juz]

uses	3rd person present
using	present participle
used	past tense & past participle

TRANSITIVE

1 to do something with a particular thing □ *They wouldn't let him use the phone.*

2 to mistreat someone in order to get an advantage □ *It is a travesty this bank uses people like pawns in a game of economic chess.*

PHRASAL VERB

use something up

to finish something so that none of it is left □ *If you use up the milk, please buy some more.*

used to

➡ See *Key Verb* entry on p. 237

wake ✪ [weik]

wakes	3rd person present
waking	present participle
woke, waked	past tense
woken	past participle

The form **waked** is used sometimes in transitive uses of the past tense.

INTRANSITIVE AND TRANSITIVE to become conscious again after being asleep, or to rouse someone from sleep

Ⓘ *She woke to find the room lit by flashing lights.*

Ⓣ *He waked me to report that my car was stolen.*

PHRASAL VERB

wake up

to stop sleeping □ *It's lovely to wake up every morning and see a blue sky.*

walk [wɑk]

walks	3rd person present
walking	present participle
walked	past tense & past participle

TRANSITIVE AND INTRANSITIVE to move forward by putting one foot in front of the other

- ⊤ *She walked two miles to school every day.*
- Ⅰ *We walked into the hall.*

PHRASAL VERB

walk out

to leave a situation suddenly in order to show that you are angry or bored
□ *Several people walked out in protest.*

warm [wɔrm]

warms	3rd person present
warming	present participle
warmed	past tense & past participle

PHRASAL VERBS

warm something up

to make something less cold □ *He blew on his hands to warm them up.*

warm up

to prepare yourself for something by doing exercises or by practicing □ *The runners were warming up for the main event.*

wash [wɑʃ]

washes	3rd person present
washing	present participle
washed	past tense & past participle

TRANSITIVE

1 to clean something using water and soap □ *She finished her dinner and washed the dishes.*

2 to clean your body using soap and water

- Ⅰ *I haven't washed for days.*
- ⊤ *She washed her face with cold water.*

PHRASAL VERBS

wash something away

If rain or floods wash away something, they destroy it and carry it away. □ *Flood waters washed away one of the main bridges.*

wash something out

to cause an event to be canceled because of rain □ *Rain washed out the entire second day's play.*

watch [wɑtʃ]

watches	3rd person present
watching	present participle
watched	past tense & past participle

> See note at **see**.

TRANSITIVE

1 to look at someone or something for a period of time □ *A man stood in the doorway, watching me.*

2 to take care of someone or something for a period of time □ *Could you watch my bags? I need to go to the bathroom.*

PHRASAL VERBS

watch out

used for warning someone to be careful
□ *You must watch out because this is a dangerous city.*

watch out for something

to pay attention so that you will notice something if it happens □ *Police warned shoppers to watch out for thieves.*

wear ✪ [wɛ°r]

wears	3rd person present
wearing	present participle
wore	past tense
worn	past participle

TRANSITIVE to have something such as clothes, shoes, or jewelry on your body
□ *He was wearing a brown shirt.*

PHRASAL VERBS

wear down

to become flatter or smoother because of rubbing against something □ *The heels on my shoes have worn down.*

wear off

to disappear slowly □ *The excitement of having a new job soon wore off.*

wear someone out

to make someone feel extremely tired

(informal) □ *The kids wore themselves out playing football.*

weave ✪ [wiv]

weaves	3rd person present
weaving	present participle
wove	past tense
woven	past participle

TRANSITIVE to make cloth by crossing threads over and under each other □ *We gathered wool and learned how to weave it into cloth.* □ *They wove and knitted their own cotton and woolen clothes.* □ *Grasses can be woven into mats or baskets.*

weep ✪ [wip]

weeps	3rd person present
weeping	present participle
wept	past tense & past participle

TRANSITIVE AND INTRANSITIVE to cry
Ⓘ *There are times when I sit down and just weep.*
Ⓣ *She wept tears of joy.*

will

➡ See *Key Verb* entry on p. 216

win ✪ [wɪn]

wins	3rd person present
winning	present participle
won	past tense & past participle

TRANSITIVE AND INTRANSITIVE
1 to do better than everyone else involved in a race, a game, or a competition
Ⓣ *The four local teams all won their games.*
Ⓘ *He does not have a chance of winning.*
2 to get a prize because you have done better than everyone else □ *The first correct entry wins the prize.*

wind ✪ [waɪnd]

winds	3rd person present
winding	present participle
wound	past tense & past participle

1 INTRANSITIVE to have a lot of bends □ *From here, the river winds through attractive countryside.*
2 TRANSITIVE to wrap something long around something else several times □ *She wound the rope around her waist.*
3 TRANSITIVE to turn part of a clock or a watch several times in order to make it work □ *Did you remember to wind the clock?*

PHRASAL VERBS

wind down

to slow down or become less active toward the end □ *Summer is beginning to wind down and it is almost time for our teachers to get back to work.*

wind something up

to finish an activity □ *Could we wind up this meeting as quickly as possible?*

wipe [waɪp]

wipes	3rd person present
wiping	present participle
wiped	past tense & past participle

TRANSITIVE
1 to rub the surface of something with a cloth to remove dirt or liquid from it □ *I'll just wipe the table.*
2 to remove dirt or liquid from something by using a cloth or your hand □ *Gary wiped the sweat from his face.*

PHRASAL VERB

wipe something out

to destroy something completely □ *The disease wiped out thousands of birds.*

work [wɜrk]

works	3rd person present
working	present participle
worked	past tense & past participle

> If you say "*I'm working in Boston,*" this suggests that the job is temporary and you may soon move to a different place. If you say "*I work in Boston,*" this suggests that Boston is your permanent place of work.

1 INTRANSITIVE to have a job and earn money for it □ *He works for the US Department of Transportation.* □ *I started working in a studio.*

used to   [jus, just STRONG jusd]

PHRASAL MODAL VERB

Used to is not a typical modal verb. Unlike the other modal verbs, it is only used in the past tense. Therefore, when it is used with the auxiliary *do* to make negatives and questions, the form of the auxiliary verb is always *did*. You use **used to** to talk about things that were done regularly in the past or that were true in the past.

> *I used to live in New Mexico.*
> *He used to deliver newspapers but he is the*
> *   publisher now.*

Negative forms

Used to has two negative forms: **did not/didn't use to**, and **used not to/usedn't to** (which is rare).

> *We didn't use to have indoor plumbing when I was a child.*
> *Alan didn't use to like children, but it's different now that he has*
> *   his own.*
> *We used not to worry much about money.*
> *Things usedn't to be so bad. What has gone wrong?*

Question forms

> *did* + **subject** + *use to* + **base form of verb**
> *"Did they use to visit you often?"—"Well, Mary used to."*
>
> ***Didn't*** *you* ***use*** *to live in Las Vegas?*

Be very careful not to confuse the structure **used to** + base form of a main verb with **_be used to_** + present participle, where **used to** means "accustomed to."

> We used to live in a condo, but we now live in a house.
> We were used to living in a condo, but we're slowly getting used to life in our new house.

Main senses

1 **Used to** is used for talking about something that happened regularly or many times in the past.

> Geraldo always used to go for a run before breakfast.
> Before we had children, we used to go on vacation several times a year.

2 **Used to** is used for talking about something that was true in the past but is no longer true.

> I used to live in Los Angeles.
> I used to like rock climbing when I was younger.

2 INTRANSITIVE to do an activity that uses a lot of your time or effort □ *You should work harder at school.*

3 INTRANSITIVE to operate correctly □ *My cell phone isn't working.*

4 INTRANSITIVE to be successful □ *Our plan worked perfectly.*

5 TRANSITIVE to use or control a machine □ *Do you know how to work the DVD player?*

PHRASAL VERBS

work out

1 to develop in a way that is good for you □ *I hope everything works out for you in Australia.*

2 to do physical exercises in order to make your body healthy □ *I work out at a gym twice a week.*

work something out

to discover the solution to a problem by thinking □ *It took me some time to work out the answer.*

would

➡ See *Key Verb* entry on p. 240

would rather

➡ See *Key Verb* entry on p. 243

wring ✪ [rɪŋ]

wrings	3rd person present
wringing	present participle
wrung	past tense & past participle

PHRASAL VERB

wring something out

to squeeze the water out of a wet piece of cloth by twisting it strongly □ *He lifted his shirt out of the sink and wrung it out.*

write ✪ [raɪt]

writes	3rd person present
writing	present participle
wrote	past tense
written	past participle

TRANSITIVE AND INTRANSITIVE

1 to use a pen or a pencil to produce words, letters, or numbers

Ⓣ *Write your name and address on a postcard and send it to us.*

Ⓘ *I'm teaching her to read and write.*

2 to create something such as a book, a poem, or a piece of music □ *She wrote articles for French newspapers.*

3 to use words to create a letter or an email

Ⓘ *She wrote to her aunt asking for help.*

Ⓣ *I have written a letter to the manager.*

PHRASAL VERBS

write something down

to record something on a piece of paper using a pen or a pencil □ *He took out a small notebook and wrote down the number.*

write someone or something off

to consider someone or something lost or worthless □ *The family wrote him off, even refusing to identify him as one of them.*

zip [zɪp]

zips	3rd person present
zipping	present participle
zipped	past tense & past participle

TRANSITIVE to use a special program to reduce the size of a computer file so that it is easier to send it to someone using the Internet □ *This is how to zip files so that you can send them via email.*

PHRASAL VERB

zip something up

to fasten something such as a piece of clothing using its zipper □ *He zipped up his jeans.*

would [wəd, STRONG wʊd]

MODAL VERB

You use **would** for making polite requests and offers, and for expressing probability. It is also used for talking about an action that was done frequently in the past, and in some conditional clauses. When you are changing sentences from direct to reported speech, **will** usually changes to **would**.

> Anna said, "Ray **will** help you."
> Anna said that Ray **would** help us.

> James said, "The car **won't** start."
> James said that the car **wouldn't** start.

Contracted forms

The contracted form of **would** is **'d**.

> We'd like to look at the garden.
> He'd be very angry if he knew about it.

The contracted negative form of **would** is **wouldn't**.

> Even if he knew about it, he wouldn't be angry.

Main senses

1 **Would** is used for making polite requests.

> Would you excuse us for a moment, Claire?
> Would you mind if I opened the window?

2 **Would** is used for making polite offers or invitations.

> *Would you like some more coffee?*
> *Would you like to come over for lunch on Saturday?*

3 **Would** is used, with *like* or *love*, as a way of saying what someone wants to do or have, or what they want to happen.

> *He asked me what I would like to do.*
> *We would like to see Mr. Brown, please.*
> *I would love to see your paintings.*

When you are talking about regrets about things you wanted but didn't have or do in the past, you use **would have**, with the past participle of *like* or *love*. Some speakers, however, express the same idea using a present base form with **would**, followed by a perfect infinitive (that is, **have** + a past participle) with *to*.

> *She would have liked to get married, but she never met the right man*
> *She would like to have gotten married, but she never met the right man.*

4 **Would** is used for talking about what someone expects or expected to happen, or to be the case.

> *I hoped that Marek would come to the meeting.*
> *I don't believe that he would do something like that.*
> *No one thought that he would resign.*

5 **Would** is used for talking about the result or effect of a possible situation.

> *It would be fun to go out to a really expensive restaurant sometime.*
> *It would be very expensive for us to go to Australia.*

6 **Would** is used for saying that someone was willing to do something. You use **would not** to show that someone refused to do something.

> *She promised that she would help us.*
> *He wouldn't say where he had been all day.*

7 **Would** is used for saying that something did not happen, often in spite of a lot of effort.

> *He pushed at the door but it wouldn't open.*
> *The wallpaper wouldn't stick to the wall.*

8 **Would** is used for talking about an activity that happened frequently in the past. Here, **would** has the same meaning as *used to*.

> *I remember when Jeff was a child; he would watch TV all day.*
> *My mother would bake on Sunday mornings.*

9 **Would** is used for saying that someone continued to do something, often something annoying, in the past. In this case, **would** is sometimes stressed.

> *John **would** keep shouting, though I asked him not to.*
> *Poor old Mary; she **would** keep forgetting things.*

10 You use **would** in conditional clauses, usually with an *if* clause, to talk about something that you think is fairly unlikely to happen.

> *If I had more money, I'd go to the festival in Montreal.*
> *If you offered me some more coffee, I wouldn't refuse.*

would rather

[ræðər/ and **had better**/həd, STRONG hæd; 'bɛtər]

PHRASAL MODAL VERB

Would rather is another way of saying *prefer*. *Had better* is used to tell someone what they should do or what you think it is wise for them to do. You use both **would rather** and **had better** with the base form of a main verb.

You use *would rather* to say what you or someone prefers to do.

> *I would rather pay by credit card.*
> *Most kids would rather play than study.*

When you are talking about the past, you add the auxiliary *have* and the past participle of the main verb.

> *I would rather have paid by credit card.*
> *They would rather have played football.*

Negative form

To form the negative, you change **would rather** to **would rather not**. You use *would rather not* to talk politely about things that people do not want to do.

> *He would rather not talk about the accident.*

Question form

To form a question, you put the subject between **would** and **rather**.

I'll order tea. Or would you rather have coffee?
Would you like to go to the movies or would you rather go
   skating?

Contracted forms

Would is shortened to **'d**, so I **would rather** becomes I**'d rather**
and I **would rather not** becomes I**'d rather not**.

   He'd rather stay at home.
   "Why are you so upset?"—"I'd rather not talk about it."

Other uses

You can also use **would rather** followed by a clause to say that
you would prefer something to happen. In the clause, you use a
form of the subjunctive (see p. 106).

   I would rather he talk to me, and not to my brother.
   Would you rather I were left out of the discussion?

You use **had better** to tell someone what you think is the best or
wisest thing for them to do, especially when it is important that
they act soon. You can also use it do indicate what you strongly
desire someone else to do or not do.

   You had better finish that report before you go on vacation.
   They had better be careful about how they approach the
      principal.

Negative form

To form the negative, you change **had better** to *had better not*. You use *had **better** **not*** to suggest what someone should avoid or be careful not to do.

> *He had better not spend all his paycheck on that stereo system.*
> *You had better not leave just now, Dad is supposed to call.*

Contracted forms

Had is shortened to **'d**, so you **had better** becomes you'**d better** and they **had better not** becomes they'**d better not**.

> *You'd better not hit me with that thing.*
> *They'd better not leave before we get there.*

Question form

Questions always use the negative form because they expect a response of "Yes." To form a question, you put the subject between **hadn't** and **better**.

> *Hadn't we better turn off all the lights before we leave?*
> *Hadn't you better make a backup copy of the file?*

Other uses

You can also use **had better** with a first-person subject to politely say no to what someone else has suggested.

> *"Won't you come to the lake with us?"— "Thanks, but I'd better get my essay done this afternoon."*

Irregular verb	Past tense	Past participle	Irregular verb	Past tense	Past participle
arise	arose	arisen	**fling**	flung	flung
awake	awoke	awoken	**fly**	flew	flown
be	was or were	been	**forbid**	forbade	forbidden
bear	bore	borne	**forecast**	forecast or forecasted	forecast or forecasted
beat	beat	beaten			
become	became	become	**forget**	forgot	forgotten
begin	began	begun	**forgive**	forgave	forgiven
bend	bent	bent	**freeze**	froze	frozen
bet	bet	bet	**get**	got	got or gotten
bind	bound	bound	**give**	gave	given
bite	bit	bitten	**go**	went	gone
bleed	bled	bled	**grind**	ground	ground
blow	blew	blown	**grow**	grew	grown
break	broke	broken	**hang**	hung or hanged	hung or hanged
breed	bred	bred			
bring	brought	brought	**have**	had	had
build	built	built	**hear**	heard	heard
burn	burned or burnt	burned or burnt	**hide**	hid	hidden
			hit	hit	hit
burst	burst	burst	**hold**	held	held
buy	bought	bought	**hurt**	hurt	hurt
cast	cast	cast	**keep**	kept	kept
catch	caught	caught	**kneel**	kneeled or knelt	kneeled or knelt
choose	chose	chosen			
cling	clung	clung	**know**	knew	known
come	came	come	**lay**	laid	laid
cost	cost	cost	**lead**	led	led
creep	crept	crept	**leap**	leaped or leapt	leaped or leapt
cut	cut	cut			
deal	dealt	dealt	**learn**	learned or learnt	learned or learnt
dig	dug	dug			
do	did	done	**leave**	left	left
draw	drew	drawn	**lend**	lent	lent
dream	dreamed or dreamt	dreamed or dreamt	**let**	let	let
			lie	lay	lain
drink	drank	drunk	**light**	lit or lighted	lit or lighted
drive	drove	driven	**lose**	lost	lost
eat	ate	eaten	**make**	made	made
fall	fell	fallen	**mean**	meant	meant
feed	fed	fed	**meet**	met	met
feel	felt	felt	**mistake**	mistook	mistaken
fight	fought	fought	**mow**	mowed	mowed or mown
find	found	found			

Irregular verb	Past tense	Past participle	Irregular verb	Past tense	Past participle
pay	paid	paid	speed	sped or	sped or
prove	proved	proved or proven		speeded	speeded
			spend	spent	spent
put	put	put	spin	spun	spun
quit	quit	quit	spit	spat or spit	spat or spit
read	read	read	spread	spread	spread
rid	rid	rid	spring	sprang	sprung
ride	rode	ridden	stand	stood	stood
ring	rang	rung	steal	stole	stolen
rise	rose	risen	stick	stuck	stuck
run	ran	run	sting	stung	stung
saw	sawed	sawn	stink	stank	stunk
say	said	said	stride	strode	strode
see	saw	seen	strike	struck	struck or stricken
seek	sought	sought			
sell	sold	sold	swear	swore	sworn
send	sent	sent	sweep	swept	swept
set	set	set	swell	swelled	swelled or swollen
sew	sewed	sewn			
shake	shook	shaken	swim	swam	swum
shear	sheared	sheared or shorn	swing	swung	swung
			take	took	taken
shed	shed	shed	teach	taught	taught
shine	shone or shined	shone or shined	tear	tore	torn
			tell	told	told
shoe	shod	shod	think	thought	thought
shoot	shot	shot	throw	threw	thrown
show	showed	shown	thrust	thrust	thrust
shrink	shrank	shrunk	tread	trod	trodden
shut	shut	shut	wake	woke or waked	woken
sing	sang	sung			
sink	sank	sunk	wear	wore	worn
sit	sat	sat	weave	wove	woven
sleep	slept	slept	weep	wept	wept
slide	slid	slid	win	won	won
sling	slung	slung	wind	wound	wound
slit	slit	slit	wring	wrung	wrung
sow	sowed	sown	write	wrote	written
speak	spoke	spoken			